T0334970

LAND!

LAND!

The Case for an Agrarian Economy

JOHN CROWE RANSOM

Edited by Jason Peters

Introduction by Jay T. Collier

University of Notre Dame Press
Notre Dame, Indiana

 A Front Porch Republic Book
Place. Limits. Liberty

University of Notre Dame Press
Notre Dame, Indiana 46556
www.undpress.nd.edu

Published in the United States of America

Library of Congress Cataloging-in-Publication Data

Names: Ransom, John Crowe, 1888–1974, author. | Peters, Jason, 1963– editor.
 | Collier, Jay T., 1974– writer of introduction.
Title: Land! : the case for an agrarian economy / John Crowe Ransom ; edited
 by Jason Peters ; introduction by Jay T. Collier.
Description: Notre Dame, Indiana : University of Notre Dame Press, [2017]
Identifiers: LCCN 2016053420 (print) | LCCN 2016055111 (ebook) | ISBN
 9780268101930 (hardcover : alk. paper) | ISBN 0268101930 (hardcover : alk.
 paper) | ISBN 9780268101954 (pdf) | ISBN 9780268101961 (epub)
Subjects: LCSH: Agriculture—Economic aspects—Southern States—History—20th
 century. | Depressions—1929—Southern States.
Classification: LCC HD1773.A5 R36 2017 (print) | LCC HD1773.A5 (ebook)
 | DDC 338.10975—dc23
LC record available at https://lccn.loc.gov/2016053420

∞ *This paper meets the requirements of ANSI/NISO Z39.48-1992*
(Permanence of Paper).

CONTENTS

EDITOR'S NOTE

A few years ago I was approached by two men previously un-
known to me, Jay Collier and Chris Hanna, who, acting upon the
advice of my friend Jeremy Beer, asked me if I knew anything
about *Land!*, an unpublished manuscript by John Crowe Ransom,
the figurehead of the Southern Agrarians. Collier and Hanna had
been made aware of the manuscript in a serendipitous meeting
with Paul Murphy, who in *The Rebuke of History* had called it "an
economic primer promoting subsistence agriculture."

I read the manuscript at a peculiar but fitting moment: in the
false peace following a federal economic stimulus program that
put more people on the road when it might have returned them
to the land. The time seemed as good as any to bring Ransom's
manuscript out of obscurity and make it available to a world
caught in what appeared then and still appears to be irremediable
economic confusion.

Ransom, noting in his day the "sad experience of capitalism"
and "the stealthy approach of a rescuer who is only socialism," ob-
jected to a false dilemma; he thought it injurious not to be able to
recognize any other option. So he proposed one, which he (and
others) called "agrarianism." "We have not canvassed our situation
thoroughly," he said, "if we fail to attend to that possibility. We
have scarcely been in a position to appreciate its excellencies until

now." Ransom wrote those words without the benefit of our vantage point: a century of prodigality and the arrival of constraints sternly telling us that we had better be capable of greater economic subtlety than we have so far been capable of.

Intending to publish *Land!* under the Front Porch Republic imprint, I went to work preparing a clean manuscript and, where appropriate, annotating it. (All the footnotes in *Land!* are mine.) Jay Collier, meanwhile, having recently finished his doctorate, put his shoulder to the task of writing an introduction.

I then thought to approach Steve Wrinn at the University of Notre Dame Press with the idea of publishing the book jointly, and we decided finally, with the blessing of Jim Tedrick at Wipf & Stock, that Notre Dame would publish *Land!* as a Front Porch Republic book. *Land!* suffers, no doubt, from the kinds of weaknesses that inevitably attend a book that has been in hiding for nearly a century. Ransom might eventually have learned from the Burley Tobacco Growers Cooperative Association that overproduction isn't inevitable, just as he might have learned from his agrarian heirs not to underestimate the knowledge and intelligence of ordinary farmers. He might have been more cautious about speaking of farming as an "industry." But I intend no rehearsal of faults here. I mean only to say how a stone got rolled away from the book's archival tomb—and maybe to place a wager, as the twilight of industrial agriculture approaches, that the resurrection will be salutary.

So it is that this book comes before the public after a long neglect. *Land!* is the title Ransom gave it; the subtitle *The Case for an Agrarian Economy* is my addition.

———

In preparing this for press I received helpful suggestions from Wendell Berry and Mark Mitchell. MaryJane Letendre, Shannon Leyva, Ginny Aumann, and Sam Dunklau transcribed the manuscript. Emma Peters helped me compare their transcription to the original. Molly Dohrmann in Special Collections and Archives at

Vanderbilt University Library helped clarify a few obscurities in the manuscript. Jay Collier and Chris Hanna deserve thanks for recognizing the importance of the book they stumbled upon and for their advice and friendship. We all received kind encouragement along the way from Ransom's granddaughters, Liz Forman and Robb Forman Dew. A grant from Augustana College provided me with release time to devote to this project, and friendship with Steve Wrinn at the University of Notre Dame Press provided me with everything else.

JASON PETERS

Williamston, Michigan
Winter 2016

INTRODUCTION

It All Turns on Sentiment: John Crowe Ransom,
Aesthetics, and Agrarian Economics

JAY T. COLLIER

In the 1930s, the United States witnessed the worst economic crisis in its history. We refer to this as the Great Depression. Along with episodes of drastic panic, the crisis produced a host of economic plans for rescuing and restructuring the economic systems in place, including all the programs rolled out by President Franklin D. Roosevelt as he sought to strike a New Deal with his fellow Americans and address the mounting unemployment problem. It was in this context that John Crowe Ransom's short economic treatise, *Land!*, was written.

But Ransom was no economist. He was a poet and literary critic. A man of letters, he taught in Vanderbilt University's English department from 1914 to 1937. From there he went to Kenyon College, where he was installed as professor of poetry and became the founding editor of the *Kenyon Review*, one of the most distinguished literary journals of the twentieth century. These are impressive credentials indeed, but not for publishing a book on economics.

How, one might ask, did Ransom ever come to write such a book? Ransom was sensitive to this question himself. In the preface to *Land!* he admitted his own limitations, but he also believed that "the amateur with all his disabilities may quite conceivably have a certain advantage over the professional; he may sometimes be able to make out a wood when the professional, who lives in it, can see only some trees."[1] Experts working within a system depend on the system for their livelihoods, which leaves them in a bad position to question the validity of the system itself. As one standing outside the guild, however, Ransom felt he was in a position to question it. He was also confident he was right.

But where did Ransom get the confidence to challenge the economic system? In order to answer that question we must know the larger story of which *Land!* is a small yet significant part. We must know the book's background, development, and eventual dissolution. We must also understand the impulse behind it and how the impulse lived on in spite of its never being published in Ransom's lifetime.

The story suggests that Ransom's experience as a poet actually conditioned him for his venture into economics. For Ransom, the higher values of life turned on sentiment, and his aesthetic commitments helped him to see the limits of the intellectual habits ascendant in his day, among them the practical and applied sciences in general and the dismal science in particular, which in Ransom's view did not keep honest ledgers.

Background

Land! was a product of Ransom's agrarian vision for the South, which he cultivated in close company with several like-minded colleagues. In the 1920s, Ransom joined a group of faculty and stu-

1. See the preface to *Land!*, 5.

dents associated with Vanderbilt University who would become known as the Fugitives. Their primary interest was neither politics nor economics but poetry and criticism.[2] It was a group that produced several important twentieth-century literary figures — Donald Davidson, Allen Tate, Robert Penn Warren, and Merrill Moore — and became the seedbed for what would become known as the New Criticism. Yet out of this tightly knit group evolved a growing concern for a Southern way of life.

During his Fugitive years, Ransom developed as a literary critic and expressed concerns about the demise of the arts. As he put it, poetry had "felt the fatal irritant of Modernity."[3] Several of his essays express his frustration with this irritant.[4] He argued that works of art "constitute the formidable reproach which a disillusioned humanity has had to cast at the scientific way of life."[5] This "scientific way of life" was more than just the ascendancy of the practical sciences over the traditional liberal arts. It was a pervasive way of approaching life that disturbed Ransom and his colleagues. For all the technological advances and conveniences of the modern era, Ransom recognized the limited ability of science to account fully for the way we experience the world. Whereas the practical bent of science focused on efficiency and production, "the experience we have when we appreciate a work of art, or when we worship God, is quite different from the scientific experience, and often it seems preferable for that very reason."[6] Yet Ransom and other Fugitives feared that science had achieved an unwarranted

2. They published a magazine called *The Fugitive* from 1922 to 1925.

3. John Crowe Ransom, "The Future of Poetry," *The Fugitive* (February 1924); also in *Selected Essays of John Crowe Ransom*, ed. Thomas Daniel Young and John Hindle (Baton Rouge: Louisiana State University Press, 1984), 27.

4. See, for instance, John Crowe Ransom, "Thoughts on the Poetic Discontent," *The Fugitive* (June 1925), or in *Selected Essays of John Crowe Ransom*, 29–32; John Crowe Ransom, "Prose: A Doctrine of Relativity," *The Fugitive* (September 1925), or in *Selected Essays of John Crowe Ransom*, 32–34.

5. John Crowe Ransom, "Classical and Romantic," *The Saturday Review of Literature*, September 14, 1929, 125.

6. Ibid., 125.

place of honor, not only in the modern mind but in all areas of modern life.

Concerned with the limits of science, Ransom devoted the greater part of his studies to aesthetics. He intended to write a book on the topic, the writing and rewriting of which ran on for several years. In it he sought to distinguish between, on the one hand, our scientific impulse to conceptualize and quantify our experiences for practical use and, on the other, the aesthetic reflex that attempts to appreciate the experience for uses that are not practical at all. Not wanting to deny the importance of science, Ransom was careful to point out its deficiency and the need for religion and the arts to help us come to terms more fully with our experiences.[7]

Ransom's book on aesthetics was never published, though he used the material in different ways. He was able to publish what he referred to as "an abridgement of some very central chapters in my aesthetic system" in *The Saturday Review of Literature*, under the title "Classical and Romantic."[8] Various themes of his study were also carried out in subsequent projects and reflected in the essays collected in *The World's Body*. One such essay, "Sentimental Exercises," examined the difference between scientific and aesthetic knowledge and the pivot that holds the two together. Whereas science prizes knowledge for efficiency, aesthetic knowledge is formed by sentimental attachments whereby we appreciate objects for the sake of their own individuality. In this essay, Ransom obviously asserted the importance of the arts for cultivating this aesthetic knowledge. Yet it is also apparent that he desired a mature

7. A synopsis of this work is given in a letter from Ransom to Tate, September 5 [1926], *Selected Letters of John Crowe Ransom*, ed. Thomas Daniel Young and George Core (Baton Rouge: Louisiana State University Press, 1985), 154–57. He called it "The Third Moment," reflecting what he saw as an order of experience: the initial moment of experience, the scientific moment of conceptualization, and the aesthetic moment of reconciliation. He contemplated the title "Studies in the Post-Scientific Function" in a letter to James A. Kirkland, October 1, 1928; see *Selected Letters of John Crowe Ransom*, 178–79.

8. Ransom to Tate, July 4, 1929, *Selected Letters of John Crowe Ransom*, 181. Ransom, "Classical and Romantic," 125–27.

society that would encourage people to form attachments to the objects of quotidian life, rather than a society in which people are hurried along merely for the sake of production.[9]

For Ransom, the aesthetic life was developed regionally—that is, with respect for place. This was clearly his approach to writing poetry and to the other arts, an approach that could adequately be described as provincial in the proper rather than in the pejorative sense of that word. Yet it became increasingly clear that he also took a regional approach to religion, politics, economics, and other aspects of life. As his aesthetic sensibilities detected the detrimental effects of modern science on culture, he also perceived that the progressive ideals of modernism were at odds with traditional principles and ways of life in the South. In the wake of the famous Scopes trial of 1925 in Dayton, Tennessee, many Southerners felt increasingly belittled in the public eye of the nation at large. Davidson reflected years later: "For John Ransom and myself, surely, the Dayton episode dramatized, more ominously than any other event easily could, how difficult it was to be a Southerner in the twentieth century."[10] Tapping in to a long-standing current of Southern pride and resentment since the War between the States and the era of Reconstruction, Ransom and his colleagues sounded the trumpet of sectionalism and embarked on a campaign for the Southern way of life that they affectionately knew as *the cause*. These Fugitive poets would soon be known as the Southern Agrarians.

Writing sometime in the spring of 1927 to Tate, who had moved to New York to write and work as an editor, Ransom described a transition that was occurring within the group:

9. John Crowe Ransom, "Sentimental Exercise," in *The World's Body* (New York: Charles Scribner's Sons, 1938), 212–32; first published as "Sentimental Exercise," *The Yale Review* 26 (December 1936): 353–68.

10. Donald Davidson, *Southern Writers in the Modern World* (Athens: University of Georgia Press, 1958), 40. Though Ransom was not a religious fundamentalist, he defended fundamentalists in the aftermath of the Scopes trial. He continued to reflect on the assault of science upon religion in Ransom, *God without Thunder: An Unorthodox Defense of Orthodoxy* (New York: Harcourt, Brace and Co., 1930).

The Fugitives met last night. The more I think about it, the more I am convinced of the excellence and the enduring vitality of our common cause. Here at Vanderbilt, which draws a lot of Old South talent, we have a very workable mine of young poets and fresh minds; always some one or two or more just clamoring for the right food and drink and society. We've got to keep on working that field; we have some perpetuals for the carry-over, like Don and me; and our cause is, we all have sensed this at about the same moment, the Old South.[11]

They pursued the idea of writing a book on Southern matters, though it was unclear what direction the book would take.[12] Tate seems to have initially envisioned a book on Southern literature, but Ransom leaned more to addressing a principled way of life. Ransom wrote to Tate in early April:

I am delighted with your idea of a book on the Old South, but have had little time to think closely upon it—our difficulty is just this: there's so little in Southern literature to point the principle. I subordinate always art to the aesthetic of life; its function is to initiate us into the aesthetic life, it is not for us the final end. In the Old South the life aesthetic was actually realized, and there are fewer object-lessons in its specific art. The old bird in the bluejeans sitting on the stump with the hound-dog at his feet knew this aesthetic, even. Our symposium of authors would be more concerned, seems to me, with making this principle clear than with exhibiting the Southern artists, who were frequently quite inferior to their Southern public in real aesthetic capacity. But

11. Ransom to Tate [Spring 1927], *Selected Letters of John Crowe Ransom*, 166.

12. Davidson first made mention of a Southern symposium in a letter to Tate, March 17, 1927; see *The Literary Correspondence of Donald Davidson and Allen Tate*, ed. John Tyree Fain and Thomas Daniel Young (Athens: University of Georgia Press, 1974), 95.

there are performances surely, to which we can point with pride, if you believe the book should be one mainly of literary criticism.[13]

Ransom had already been working on an essay that he called "Pioneering on Principle," which he passed along to Tate as an example of the sort of material he felt would best fit their symposium.[14] He would use this article several times over the next few years in order to forward the cause. For instance, Ransom "reduced and compressed it to a rather provocative belligerent form" and tried to get it published as "The South—Old or New?" *The Nation* declined to publish it in the spring of 1927, but Ransom was finally able to get it published in the *Sewanee Review* in 1928.[15] An expanded version of the article was published in *Harper's Monthly Magazine* in 1929 under the title "The South Defends Its Heritage."[16] There was talk of an offer to have an even further expanded version published in the Today and Tomorrow series of booklets, though such a piece never materialized.[17] And when the group's idea for a symposium finally came together, Ransom adapted the essay yet again. It ran as "Reconstructed but Unregenerate" in *I'll Take My Stand*.[18]

The group book project did not take off immediately. Though there was initial interest on the part of Ransom, Tate, and

13. Ransom to Tate, April 3 and 13, 1927, *Selected Letters of John Crowe Ransom*, 173.

14. Ibid., 174.

15. Ransom to Tate, June 25 [1927], *Selected Letters of John Crowe Ransom*, 175. John Crowe Ransom, "The South—Old or New?" *Sewanee Review* (April 1928): 139–47.

16. John Crowe Ransom, "The South Defends Its Heritage," *Harper's Monthly Magazine*, June 1929, 108–18. Ransom was not happy with the title *Harper's* had given it, preferring instead the title "Reconstructed but Unregenerate." See Ransom to Tate, July 4, 1929, *Selected Letters of John Crowe Ransom*, 182.

17. Ransom to Tate, July 4, 1929, *Selected Letters of John Crowe Ransom*, 182.

18. Twelve Southerners, *I'll Take My Stand: The South and the Agrarian Tradition* (New York: Harper & Brothers, 1930).

Davidson, it soon fell neglected in 1927 and 1928. But in February 1929, Davidson wrote a letter to Tate, who was now in Paris on a Guggenheim fellowship, seeking for the group to redouble its efforts. He not only solicited Tate's help in reviving the book project, but he also cast a larger vision of influence with a dream of starting a Southern magazine. Yet in the midst of his visionary efforts, Davidson voiced his pessimism about the whole scheme. "Economics, government, politics, machinery—all such forces are against us. With the issue of prosperity before everybody's eyes, Southerners get excited about nothing else—except religion."[19]

Over the next few months, the trio renewed the cause with vigor. They discussed matters of organization, contributors, and publishers. They also deliberated greater structural concerns for the cause, such as starting an academic society, placing essays in various journals, starting a magazine or newspaper, and connecting with young literary groups at colleges.[20] The Agrarians had a renewed sense of focus, a plan, and plenty of energy. But was that enough to overcome Davidson's concern about the soporific effect of prosperity? By fall the economic scene underwent a noticeable change that would alleviate some of that pessimism. Davidson wrote to Tate on October 26, 1929: "The terrific industrial 'crises' now occurring almost daily in North Carolina give present point to all the line of thinking and argument that we propose to do. I don't know whether you have read of these or not. It is enough to say that hell has pretty well broken loose, and the old story of labor fights is being repeated. It all means more ammunition for us."[21] On October 29, 1929, the U.S. stock market crashed, and the country found itself reeling under what would become known

19. Davidson to Tate, February 5, 1929, *Literary Correspondence*, 221.

20. Davidson to Tate, July 29, 1929, *Literary Correspondence*, 226–29; Tate to Davidson, August 10, 1929, *Literary Correspondence*, 229–33; Davidson to Tate, August 20, 1929, *Literary Correspondence*, 233–34.

21. Davidson to Tate, October 26, 1929, *Literary Correspondence*, 235.

as the Great Depression. By the end of the year, Davidson declared that "the time is ripe."[22]

The Agrarians hurried to finish the book, secured Harper & Brothers as a publisher, and rejoiced to see the book published in the fall of 1930. Under the title *I'll Take My Stand: The South and the Agrarian Tradition*, the book distinguished between what its contributors saw as agrarian and industrial ways of life. *I'll Take My Stand* received wide recognition upon publication, though many of the reviews were negative. It was received unfavorably by such Northern critics as the influential H. L. Mencken.[23] Yet from the beginning Ransom had recognized that their greatest battles would be against progressive-leaning Southerners. As he had written to Tate in the spring of 1927, "Our fight is for survival; and it's got to be waged not so much against the Yankees as against the exponents of the New South."[24] And, as predicted, opposition came from their fellow Southerners. Over the next year, Ransom engaged in a number of debates to defend the Southern way of life advanced in the book.[25] Although they received significant opposition to their cause, the Agrarians had developed a platform and were being heard.

LAND!

In the wake of *I'll Take My Stand*, economics became a main source of tension between Ransom and his New South opponents. Ransom's agrarianism stood opposed to the capitalism of a predominantly industrialized society. But whereas *I'll Take My Stand* addressed the multifaceted cultural problems related to indus-

22. Davidson to Tate, December 29, 1929, *Literary Correspondence*, 246.

23. H. L. Mencken, "Uprising in the Confederacy," *American Mercury*, March 1931, 379–81.

24. Ransom to Tate [Spring 1927], *Selected Letters of John Crowe Ransom*, 166.

25. See Davidson, *Southern Writers in the Modern World*, 46–50.

trialism, Ransom thought the book lacked a significant economic argument for an agrarian return. As he says in the preface to *Land!*, he saw the need for an "economic sequel to the group-book."[26] *Land!* would be that sequel, and its purpose would be to assess the unemployment crisis and to name its principal cause: the problem of overcapitalization. As Ransom observed, the percentage of farmers had severely dropped over the years as people vacated the countryside for jobs in the cities. With the unemployment crisis underway, he proposed that people return to the land: there was plenty of work to do on the farm. The book would also review commonly proposed solutions to the Great Depression, ranging from capitalist fixes to socialist schemes. Yet it would distinguish the agrarian program from both capitalism and socialism, arguing for the existence of a completely different economic option from the two prevailing systems. It was a system that would promote self-sufficiency and local interests, prioritizing farm life over manufacturing.

Inasmuch as he "debated and discussed and even wrote that topic" during the winter of 1931, Ransom concluded, "I might as well 'capitalize' my efforts into a book and get it behind me." Ransom had been awarded a Guggenheim scholarship for the 1931–32 academic year, so bringing a bit of closure to his foray into economics would allow him better focus on his poetic calling. He proposed the book idea to Harcourt under the title "Capitalism and the Land" and hoped to finish writing it that summer before going overseas.[27]

Summer ended and the book was not complete. Once in England, Ransom continued to work on the book, and he recruited Tate to serve as his stateside literary agent. Harcourt had declined his proposal, and, as appears from a letter to Tate, Scribner's had

26. Preface to *Land!*, 4. Shortly after the publication of *I'll Take My Stand*, Ransom's attempt to get the group to sign on to a positive economic project apparently did not succeed; see Ransom to Tate [December, 1930], *Selected Letters of John Crowe Ransom*, 201.

27. Ransom to Louis Untermeyer, July 7, 1931, *Selected Letters of John Crowe Ransom*, 203.

too. With two rejections on the proposal, Ransom submitted part of the manuscript to Harper & Brothers with an offer to have a complete manuscript by January 15, 1932. Ransom instructed Harper & Brothers to send it to Tate if they decided not to publish it, with the idea that Tate could help pitch it to other publishers.[28] Harper declined the manuscript.

As the New Year rolled around, Ransom continued to work diligently on his economic project. A small light of hope began to shine when *The New Republic* published an article from his labors under the title "The State and the Land."[29] With a little wind in his sail, Ransom approached Harcourt once again with a reworked book manuscript, to be titled simply *Land!* In May 1932 Ransom received a rejection letter from Harcourt. Discouraged, he let Tate know of his reticence to send it to any other publishers. He wanted Tate to see the manuscript in its present form, which he felt was much stronger than earlier versions, and he even considered having Tate propose the book to Macmillan. However, Ransom started to weary under the strain of negotiating the manuscript from overseas, and his confidence as a lay economist became shaky. Ransom lamented,

> the economic subject matter shifts so rapidly that an utterance becomes an anachronism before it can get to print. Don't peddle it any further, therefore. It may be that in the fall I can take it up again profitably. But it may be, on the other hand, that my kind of economics won't do, and that I'd better stick to poetry and aesthetics. I've learned a lot of economics lately, too! But I must confess I haven't the economist's air, flair, style, method, or whatnot.[30]

28. Ransom to Tate, November 23 [1931], *Selected Letters of John Crowe Ransom*, 206.

29. John Crowe Ransom, "The State and the Land," *The New Republic*, February 17, 1932, 8–10. See appendix herein.

30. Ransom to Tate, May 19 [1932], *Selected Letters of John Crowe Ransom*, 208.

Nevertheless, not all was lost. Whereas Harper & Brothers had also declined the book at an earlier stage, they now agreed to publish part of his work as an article in the July issue of *Harper's Monthly Magazine*. It was given the title "Land! An Answer to the Unemployment Problem."[31]

When Ransom returned to the United States in the fall, his hopes of recovering the book project came to a decisive end. Writing of his dissatisfaction, Ransom told Tate:

> My poor book is nearly a total loss—I don't like it. It would have been a passable book published a year ago. Several publishers nearly took it. Within these next ten days I will have kicked it into the incinerator or else taken a grand new start and started over on a new outline together. The latter course would relieve my system, and I am getting a little bit gone on my new (hypothetical) approach.[32]

As a book project, *Land!* had come to an end. Ransom gave up on publishing it. And his saying that in a few days he would have "kicked it into the incinerator" caused many later scholars to believe he had in fact destroyed the manuscript altogether.[33] Ransom seems to have had a penchant for feeding the fire with old unwanted materials. For instance, in the preface to *The World's Body*, he tells of how he had recently "consigned to the flames" his rejected manuscript on the aesthetics of poetry, which he had

31. John Crowe Ransom, "Land! An Answer to the Unemployment Problem," *Harper's Monthly Magazine*, July 1932, 216–24. This essay consists of most of chapter 1, four paragraphs from chapter 4, and some additional material that is not a part of *Land!*

32. Ransom to Tate, October 25 [1932], *Selected Letters of John Crowe Ransom*, 210–11.

33. Thomas Daniel Young, *Gentleman in a Dustcoat: A Biography of John Crowe Ransom* (Baton Rouge: Louisiana State University Press, 1976), 241; Michael O'Brien, *The Idea of the American South, 1920–1941* (Baltimore: Johns Hopkins University Press, 1979), 128; see *Selected Letters of John Crowe Ransom*, 211n6; Paul K. Conkin, *The Southern Agrarians* (Nashville: Vanderbilt University Press, 2001), 101.

worked on so hard before and alongside the agrarian project.[34] So it is reasonable that his remark to Tate led people to assume the manuscript no longer existed. But although Ransom's plans for publishing *Land!* had gone up in metaphorical smoke, the manuscript itself evaded the literal flames.

And although *Land!* was aborted as a book project, Ransom's comments to Tate indicated an alternative approach that would allow him to address the topic in a new way. He did not spell out that new way in the letter to Tate, but his publishing efforts over the next five years demonstrated that he was not quite finished addressing agrarian economic concerns. Rather than write a book, Ransom wrote a number of articles for various publications. These articles were not excerpted material from the book but fresh pieces that addressed the issues in different ways. However, rather than sticking to strict economics, as he had in *Land!*, Ransom infused these essays with aesthetic and regionalist concerns. The original book project might have been abandoned, but it took several years of publishing articles to clear his system of his agrarian fervor.[35]

THE RESIGNED POET

By 1936, Ransom expressed concern over his involvement in the agrarian cause. All during the years of advocating agrarianism, he had simultaneously maintained his interest in writing poetry and criticism. For a while his agrarian and poetic output served as complementary projects in his defense of the humane tradition against a modernist society. But he came to a point at which he feared the

34. Ransom, *The World's Body*, vii.
35. See "Happy Farmers," *American Review* 1, no. 5 (October 1933): 513–35; "A Capital for the New Deal," *American Review* 2, no. 2 (December 1933): 129–42; "The Aesthetic of Regionalism," *American Review* 2, no. 3 (January 1934): 290–310; "Regionalism in the South," *New Mexico Quarterly* (May 1934): 108–13; "The South Is a Bulwark," *Scribner's Magazine*, May 1936, 299–303; "What Does the South Want?" *Virginia Quarterly Review* (Spring 1936): 180–94; "The Unequal Sections," *The Saturday Review*, December, 18, 1937, 6–7.

agrarian cause was subverting his calling as a poet. Not that the two projects were antithetical. But he was being emotionally consumed by the project in a way that was compromising his literary aims. Ransom wrote to Tate about how *"patriotism* is eating at *lyricism"*; *"patriotism* has nearly eaten me up," he said, "and I've got to get out of it."[36] A few years earlier Ransom thought he recognized a similar problem in Davidson, though he could not see at that time how it would come to eat him up as well. He once wrote to Tate, "You know, our rebel doctrines are good for all [of] us but Don, and very doubtful there, because they are flames to his tinder."[37] Now he found himself eaten up and burned out. There had been in Ransom an aesthetic impulse that carried him into his venture in agrarian economics, but when he sensed that the extended project began to compromise his commitments to poetry, he chose to regroup and concentrate solely on his artistic calling.

Ransom struggled with his patriotic dilemma over the next year. For the sake of his sanity and career he looked for projects that would keep his mind and hands busy with literary concerns. For instance, he discussed with Tate the idea of starting an American academy of letters.[38] And writing to Edwin Mims, chair of the English department at Vanderbilt, Ransom gave assurance that he had lately "gone almost entirely into pure literary work."[39] Making that transition was not easy. Ransom confessed to Tate that he found himself "lapsing occasionally" back into the agrarian project because there were still things he felt he had to get off his chest.[40] He was working on an article that took the agrarian project in a more political direction. He told Tate that he was "signing off

36. Ransom to Tate, September 17, 1936, *Selected Letters of John Crowe Ransom*, 217 (emphasis in original).

37. Ransom to Tate, October 25 [1932], *Selected Letters of John Crowe Ransom*, 209.

38. Ransom to Tate, September 17, 1936, *Selected Letters of John Crowe Ransom*, 217–19.

39. Ransom to Edwin Mims, June 8, 1937, *Selected Letters of John Crowe Ransom*, 223.

40. Ransom to Tate, March 11, 1937, *Selected Letters of John Crowe Ransom*, 221.

but a little by degrees" and described the article as his "last act of patriotism."[41] Ransom sent the article to Seward Collins for publication in the *American Review*, which went defunct a few months later, and Ransom's article never appeared. But the agrarian fever proved persistent. At one point Ransom remarked to Tate that "there'll never be complete immunity for any good man from patriotism" and that they might better commit to "keep out of a *repetitive* patriotism at least."[42] But as much as the fire burned within him, its dying seemed inevitable. His final published agrarian piece appeared at the end of 1937. It was a review for the *Saturday Review* of Walter Prescott Webb's *Divided We Stand*. He used the piece as a platform to encourage the southern and western regions of the United States to take a political stand against the "economic dominion of the North."[43]

What made the year 1937 a decisive break is that Ransom had indeed diverted his attention to significant literary concerns that would solidify his career as a leading literary critic. That year he wrote an important article entitled "Criticism, Inc.," which called for a more precise and systematic practice of literary criticism.[44] He worked this article and a number of his previous articles on poetry into a book, *The World's Body*, one purpose of which was to set down precisely what it is that poetry does for us that the sciences cannot. Also in 1937, Ransom relocated to Gambier, Ohio, taking the job of professor of poetry at Kenyon College. Removed from Nashville and expected to lead Kenyon's English department to distinction, Ransom found little to no incentive for delving back into the Southern agrarian project.

Having retreated from the front lines of the agrarian cause, Ransom sought to maintain his fight against modernity's ill

41. Ransom to Tate, April 6, 1937, *Selected Letters of John Crowe Ransom*, 222.

42. Ransom to Tate, June 17, 1937, *Selected Letters of John Crowe Ransom*, 224.

43. Ransom, "The Unequal Sections," 7.

44. John Crowe Ransom, "Criticism, Inc.," *Virginia Quarterly Review* 13, no. 4 (1937): 586–602.

influence but focused it more singularly in the arena of literary criticism. He came to accept the agrarian program as a lost cause, but he never lost the aesthetic concerns that carried him into it. In "Art and the Human Economy" he reproached those who still proposed agrarianism, but he also spoke of an "agrarian nostalgia" as "a mode of repentance not itself to be repented."[45] The project allowed the Fugitives to recognize something that was being lost in the rapid progress of industrialization. And although witnessing a return to an agrarian way of life that preserved aesthetic values within its very economic system no longer seemed possible, Ransom concluded that they were better suited to infusing into the modern world, by means of the arts, as much aesthetic sensibility as was possible. It was a retreat from agrarianism as an economic program, but not from the sentiments that had given rise to it.

———————

This publication of *Land!*, after all these years, resurrects for us the story of a poet temporarily turned lay economist. Ransom was acutely aware of the way that a modern progressive spirit was revolutionizing the South. All of the emphasis on a scientific push for efficiency had altered an older, more traditional agrarian economic system—a system with a simple aesthetic quality built into it. As Ransom and his colleagues challenged the industrial way of life by advocating agrarianism, and as the economic crisis of the Great Depression gave them a greater platform for their cause, they also recognized that their agrarian proposal would have to stand up under economic scrutiny if Southern society were to consider such a return a viable option. Thus, *Land!* was a strictly economic justification for a Southern agrarianism. Feeling out of his element in ever-changing economic times, Ransom failed to bring *Land!* to publication. Instead, he lobbied agrarian economics from the vantage point of the critic, touting its aesthetic advantage and its greater ability to preserve human dignity. Finally, when that

45. John Crow Ransom, "Art and the Human Economy," *The Kenyon Review* 7, no. 4 (1945): 687.

cause seemed completely lost, he resigned himself to the life of a diligent literary critic, hoping that the arts would preserve the aesthetic life he longed to see maintained.

In this story we can see that the very thing that drove Ransom to even attempt writing an economic treatise was his ever abiding concern for developing the aesthetic side of life. This is what explains the oddity—if "oddity" is the right word, for Ransom *was* a man of letters in the old sense—of the poet-turned-economist. He ventured outside of his expertise in order to give an economic justification for a more aesthetically responsible way of life. At that moment in American history everything seemed to turn on economics. Ransom recognized this, but his foray into economics was not for the love of it as an economist. Rather, his stint as an economist turned on the fact that he valued a society where daily production allowed people to form local attachments and enjoy the everyday aspects of a life well lived. The advantage of a self-sufficient farm, he wrote in *Land!*, is that "it offers expression to Man Thinking as well as to Man Laboring."[46] He could not expect economists of his day to articulate the economic sense of agrarianism, for they could not see the forest through the trees, so he sought to learn enough economics to do the job himself. And what led him to do it? One could say that it all turned on sentiment.

46. See chapter 4 herein, 105.

LAND!

The Case for an Agrarian Economy

PREFACE

I have undertaken in this book to show the economic import of an agrarian movement. But to what movement do I refer? Alas, I am justifying a movement that does not yet exist on any conscious or concerted scale. It is my belief that such a movement must now be recommended by anybody who is sensitive to the logic of economic events, and perhaps that it is even to be predicted; that is about all.

It is not quite all. In the fall of 1930 appeared a book entitled *I'll Take My Stand: The South and the Agrarian Tradition.*[1] It had twelve authors, of whom I was one. The essays, as was natural, repeated each other to some extent, so that the book's real content may have been less than its volume would indicate. Perhaps its chief significance lay in the fact that here were twelve men of presumptive intelligence standing together on some principles rather at variance with the orthodox doctrines of the American economic society. And their peculiar variation was not in the direction of something that was new but of something that was old. They

---

1. First published by Harper & Brothers (New York) in what Louis D. Rubin, Jr., called "a modest edition that was subsequently permitted to go out of print." See Rubin's introduction to the edition published by Louisiana State University Press (Baton Rouge, 1977), xi.

named it the "agrarian tradition." They were aware that this had nearly passed out of effective existence, but they believed in recovering it.

How it could be recovered was not, naturally, set forth in much detail. Everybody rather indicated that there was economic reason for an agrarian return and almost nobody elaborated the argument with any circumstance. The book consisted in so many overtures to the spirit of man, so many appeals to his taste.

So I have written the present little book. I have not applied for an imprimatur from the group, which is neither an ecclesiastical nor a political organization. But I shall be happy if my colleagues or the public find in it a sort of economic sequel to the group-book.

A book about a reform must have a villain, a *bête noire*. In our symposium the beast's name was "industrialism." It was the right name for the character playing opposite agrarianism, which was defined both as a way of laboring and as a way of enjoying life. For industrialism connotes both our now highly specialized jobs and positions, and also those pretty mechanisms and packaged commodities that give us our joy as consumers.

In the present book the villain is generally called "capitalism," but he is the same character. Industrial with respect to the way he appeals to our senses and touches our spirits, capitalistic with respect to the source of his power and revenues. Capitalism is the economic organization, industrialism is the kind of culture which it supports. In this book I am talking economics and not culture.

I might add that the piece is not a tragedy. I would not want to put my villain to death if I knew how. I propose to rescue some unfortunate people from his clutches and then leave him to his own devices.

———————

I feel the same embarrassment that I felt in contributing to the other book: do I write as a Southerner or as an American? I hope it is possible to be both at the same time, though some of our critics have told us to the contrary. I write as an economist of some sort believing that we are now obliged to rebuild in a decent fashion our agrarian communities. But I cannot help observing that the agrarian communities of the South, though they have declined sadly, are still the best-preserved specimens to be found in the Union. Those blocs of States usually designated as the South Atlantic, the South Central, and the Southwestern contain a larger farming population than do all the other States put together. In the South there is still a sectional pride attaching to its old agrarian traditions, and this deserves to be used rather than abused. I hope for an agrarian revival in the South, but that is not nearly good enough: I would like to see the rehabilitation of an agrarian theory in our national thinking, and a Southern agrarianism will depend on it for success just as much as that of any other region.

Nothing of importance in this book applies solely or peculiarly to the South.

———————

I am not professionally or technically an economist. In saying this I shall be anticipating a good many of my critics. Nevertheless I shall not pretend to be prostrated when I say it with a sense of my incompetence. The amateur with all his disabilities may quite conceivably have a certain advantage over the professional; he may sometimes be able to make out a wood when the professional, who lives in it, can see only some trees.

———————

I am indebted to the John Simon Guggenheim Memorial Foundation for the leisure in which, as a Guggenheim Fellow staying in England, I have done a large part of the writing of this book.

I also owe acknowledgements to *Harper's Magazine* and the *New Republic* for the use of material which I have already published under their copyright.[2]

2. "Land! An Answer to the Unemployment Problem," *Harper's Magazine*, July 1932, 216–24; "The State and the Land," *New Republic*, February 17, 1932, 8–10.

And now for a quick impressionistic picture of our economic landscape.

Something dreadful is happening to the Western world, and that includes even America, once locally known as God's own country. We have wealth, yet we are materially distressed, and what is more we are panicky at heart. It is said that we suffer from a "depression," but what does that mean? It is like the names that have been given to some of the diseases of the body; they do not define the condition, they do not tell anybody specifically what virus to attack. We were apparently enjoying a gorgeous state of health and now suddenly we are sick. Yet the regime of our economic life seemed sound; the theory behind it was perfect.

Here was the theory. Every one of us was providentially equipped with a special service which he could perform for others and in return for which he could expect to obtain their services. It was as if we were so many atoms of humanity who yet were not meant exactly for the solitary state but for a communicating fellowship. The butcher swapped wares with the baker. The atoms assisted one another; they were economic atoms.

But that does not begin to describe the intricacy of our economic pattern. There was not only the simple order of uncompounded services, such as the loaf baked in the one-man bake-shop. There were services that were performed, and could only be performed, by large numbers of atoms in concert; that is, by molecules. The wares put up for exchange were mass-products or molecular products strictly. They were the work of companies, corporations, cartels, and came out of factories and industrial plants. The picture of the world in 1929, so far as Americans could see it, was not the picture of so many separate point-like economic atoms but the picture of congeries of atoms, or molecules, which were already big and growing always bigger. The atoms had gone molecular.

What was the molecular organization like? A factory was a marvel of ingenuity for turning out wares, and at the same time it was somebody's large physical property. It had an owner-atom who was responsible for the ingenuity, and it was just as much a private possession as a bake-shop. Ownership had been secured by a series of private transactions, and that again was the way it was operated. The owner-atom invited into it many worker-atoms who consented each to work according to his directions. Then by other private transactions he took the factory's products and exchanged them. The worker-atoms had not flown by some mechanical compulsion into place within the molecules; they had elected the place.

The molecules were not organized for fun, nor in order to be aesthetic objects. Out of the molecule came services which were proportionately at least as large as the services of the uncompounded atoms, and in fact much larger; and then there came back services for the sustenance of the member atoms in their turn. The real living creatures in the world were still only the atoms. They grouped into molecules for the sake of their own convenience and at the bright suggestion of the owner-atoms; in doing which they conferred no life on the molecules, nor did they cease to be themselves constitutionally atoms and nothing but atoms. If the advantage of the molecular grouping disappeared, the molecule dissolved, for the atoms naturally returned to their separateness; and probably soon decided to enter some molecules somewhere else. And as for the smartness of the owner-atoms who discovered and applied the theory of molecularity, it could scarcely stray off after fantastic and unprofitable objectives altogether. The owner-atom had at least two checks upon his imagination: he had to satisfy the consumer-atoms with the services that his molecule issued, and he had to satisfy the worker-atoms with a fair share of the services that came back in return. If he failed in either particular, he failed altogether, he had to drop out of the molecular game, his great name as the founder of a molecular establishment was forgotten, and somebody else took his place who could make himself more useful.

The more familiar name of the molecular structure is capitalism. The terms I have used are perhaps crude ones but I think they will do for sketching in outline. Capitalism means plants and factories with owners and employers; but it rests everywhere on private consent, and its benefits if it has any are to private persons. The capitalistic enterprises are molecules, and in theory it would seem that they cannot operate to the hurt of the atoms, that they cannot really go wrong.

But they have gone wrong. The novelty is that they have gone wrong in great numbers, and all at the same time. They are at a stand-still, waiting to see whether they will disintegrate or pick up again. And in the meantime every private atom connected with them is involved in their distress. The capitalistic or molecular order is threatened with extinction. The worker-atoms are beginning to shout, Down with the owner-atoms, who have managed our molecules so badly; let us run the molecules ourselves!

Strangely enough, I have not heard of them shouting, though this too might not be a bad piece of logic: Away with molecules, they are too dangerous! Doubtless worker-atoms have grown so habituated to working within molecules that they can scarcely conceive of any other way of working; and so fond of the peculiar services rendered by molecules that they cannot imagine themselves doing without them.

But is it not possible that our atoms have simply gone too deeply into molecularity? Possibly they overestimated the benefits, seeing that they certainly underestimated the dangers. After all, atoms were living in good health before molecules were ever heard of. It is clearly going to be hard for the atoms to save themselves now by saving the molecules in any form. It may also be hard for them to revert to the condition of being uncompounded atoms. But they might be interested in the proposition that this latter course is easier than they have been led to suppose, and that it is worth a try.

Of fundamental importance of any age is the way it tries to secure the economic welfare of its atoms. There has just been conducted a long experiment with molecularity under which they fared more and more brilliantly, till suddenly now they find themselves coming more and more to grief. Perhaps the issue for the new age to determine is: Molecularity or Atomicity?

At any rate, something will have to be done; or so I have heard. The Governor of the Bank of England is said to have told the Governor of the Bank of France: "Unless drastic measures are taken to save it, the capitalistic system throughout the civilized world will be wrecked within a year. I should like that prediction to be filed for future reference."[3] What did he mean by drastic? Since he spoke these words, Mr. Hoover has declared a moratorium on international settlements, and Britain has gone off gold and put in a Tory government and a tariff. The year has passed, and the capitalistic system is thought to be breathing a little easier but one is not sure. Were these remedies enough?

—John Crowe Ransom

3. Montagu Collet Norman in a letter to Clément Moret, which appeared in the press in the summer of 1931. For a brief discussion, see Liaquat Ahamed, *Lords of Finance* (New York: Penguin, 2009), 5.

Chapter 1

HOMELESS PEOPLE
AND VACANT LAND

Man's inhumanity to man—resounding and portentous phrase—
need not, I imagine, describe our inevitable or usual human relations, as Malthus[1] might have thought it did if he had been asked
to pass judgment. But it is terrifyingly apt at describing our present
ones. A certain economic practice has brought us to a condition
where we are competing with each other for survival. We are in
business, and there is not enough business to go round. All must
take part in this game of economic competition, not merrily but
perforce, and nobody can win until somebody loses. The stakes
are no longer the naive delights of power, glory, finery, and sump-
tuary extravagance, but the means of bare subsistence. The competitive condition is not less dreary because it is universal. Nor is
our conduct the less murderous because we do not mean any
harm, and bear no particular malice against our competitors. We
are engaged in a kind of civil war, though hostilities have not been
declared, and scarcely even intended.

1. Thomas Robert Malthus (1766–1834), English cleric and economist,
author of *An Essay on the Principle of Population*, which argued that population
would outpace the earth's capacity to sustain it.

I suppose this way of putting it is hardly too strong in April of 1932. But I can be much more specific, and recount some commonplace bits of fact.

I live in a moderately well-to-do residential section of a fair-sized city. At the top of my street lives an undertaker, who has a "mortuary establishment" downtown. His business is doing badly, and he cannot hold out much longer. But it is not because people are not dying at a due and healthy rate; it is because there are suddenly far too many undertakers, and they could not support themselves on a normal death rate; they would require a series of plagues.

Very quick would be the answer which some earlier society, with its simpler ideas, would make to the undertaker's complaint: Why does he not then try some other business? But since he himself has not been long an undertaker, it is certain that he must have thought of that, that his mind is open to the idea of changing his occupation again. As he looks over our neighborhood, however, or even our city, he cannot find that the men in the other businesses are doing particularly better than he is. *All the businesses seem to be overmanned and overproductive, and there is no business for him to turn to.* It is a new condition in American life, the rather tragic culmination of an economic development that has been vaster and more rapid than anything like it in history.

The undertaker is only a sample. An insurance salesman lives near; he has almost gone out of business, and is living on his "renewals." Insurance is still being bought, though not on the scale of five years ago; but five years ago, and previously, there were coming into being too many insurance companies with too many salesmen, and there is simply not the trade to accommodate them all. Then there are several merchants, unanimous in reporting that they are not getting business, and times are very hard. They are the victims of an economy that has set up too many mercantile establishments, and allocated to their personnel too many shrewd, capable, honest men. There are also several sorts of salaried men in our community: managers, travelling salesmen, department heads, technicians. All are worrying. They do not know when they will be laid off. They are miserably aware that their service is scarcely paying for itself, that their employers have lost too much business under the condition of overcompetition and oversupply.

I myself am a college teacher, and I still have my job, but doubtless it is at the expense of a good many threadbare and desperate scholars who would like to take it from me. I know such men. There are far too many of us trying to make scholarship pay. And as for school-teachers, the teacher-training institutions of my State have been turning them out for the last ten years in impossible numbers. There cannot be found positions for them all unless the present teachers who did not go to college are discharged for their benefit; and when it comes to the question whether the old teachers or the new teachers are to become the supernumeraries of the economic order and retire into economic darkness, the political economist has no preference whatever.

There are other professional men in our section—doctors, a dentist, lawyers, preachers. All are trying to cut the throats of their competitors. Or trying to strangle them, I had better say; for they are rarely bloodthirsty by nature. Many of them preferred professional life to business precisely because they assumed that the competitive technique would not have to be so ruthless. But the professions are just as overcrowded as the businesses, and the alternative before their members is to fight for a man's share of the limited patronage or waste away of inanition.

Beyond my section is the suburb where reside the big men who run big business. Their story is like our story but on a grander scale. The manufacturer is manufacturing only by fits and starts. His plant is like nearly half the plants in his industry: superfluous. The banker lives in fear of his economic life. Banking is a pretty business, and it is not strange that too many men, carrying too many capital funds, have entered it. Unfortunately it has been the recent fashion for banks which were having a hard struggle individually to merge, and to cut down their personnel, and some of them have not quite lasted until the merger could be completed. And what of the *rentiers*—the privileged ones who live on Easy

Street itself, and whose economic function consists in clipping coupons from gilt-edged securities?[2] The securities have too often turned out to be of no better composition than the edges. So these folk are retrenching from their former scale of living as their incomes have dropped off, and some of them are barely intact, economically speaking. For the *rentier* has his enemies too, though not mean-spirited personal ones, I hope; he has competitors, who are all the *rentiers* everywhere that have poured capital into productive investment until none of it produces as it should. As the tradesman and the manufacturer and the banker suffer so he must suffer, because it is his money that has set them up, and his money that must be lost when the business goes to pieces.

In the opposite direction from this rich-man's suburb, toward the city, is the shabby district where the large families of day-to-day laborers lead their hand-to-mouth existence. Nobody can now find any gloss to spread over that picture! The laborers want labor, but the labor is insufficient, and so the hand of each is in effect raised against his neighbor. The laborer's distress is cruder and more obvious than that of other members of the economic community. His position is exactly the same in the respect that, when his own particular occupation fails him, there is no other for him to enter.

Surplus of production, fierce competition, crowded occupations: the condition is so prevalent that it forms for us a sort of economic atmosphere; we feel it and breathe it everywhere we go. In such a situation there might be the makings of revolution and violence but for one consideration: all the ranks suffer alike, and there is no particular direction in which to attack. There is no villain nor set of villains in this drama. There are not even any great fools, for it is hard to smell out precisely where the folly lies, and it is evidently a kind of folly that has infected us all about the same.

2. From the French, *rentier*: "A person who derives his or her income from property or investment" (OED).

But we are loath to accept that as a picture of our "normal" economic condition and, without knowing precisely what is the matter, we are inclined to believe that it will give place sooner or possibly later to a picture which is bright and pleasant. To an uncertain extent that must be true. Let us hope it as hard as we can. Evidently our hope is mainly the not very rational one that, since good times and bad times seem to succeed each other in alternation, good times are coming back.

Good times consist in occupation for all; an economic function for everybody; it is the first desideratum of sound political economy. It is entirely too possible that we shall not see it realized again in our time. We look forward in fear, and we look backward in fondness, and ask ourselves, Why should it not obtain again as it obtained before? It is necessary to see how it obtained the last time, and what was really happening to make it obtain then, and to make it unapt to obtain quickly again.

The abundant occupation which offered itself in the flush times just before the crash was not an entirely sound condition. The event proves it, and a little economic logic will explain it. The occupation was abundant, but some of it was of a sort that could not last and must soon be withdrawn. This precarious or temporary occupation fell into at least three large groups.

(1) There was first the occupation of those who were working for businesses that were really on the point of breaking but did not dare to stop and see. They were producing goods that were increasingly failing to get sold, and cluttering up the market. They kept going in the hope that things would be better for them tomorrow. Monetary conditions helped them to keep going. Prices were rising, and tended to reimburse them each season for the costs of production in the previous season; these costs had been incurred on a lower price scale but they were nevertheless heavy because they had to cover wasted or unused production. If the businesses required to make loans to continue operation, they could probably do it, for credit was plentiful. But the longer they

kept going the further they were getting behind and the greater would be the crash when they stopped.

These businesses were the weaker or "marginal" businesses in industries which on the whole were overproductive; and in being overproductive it is to be understood that they were simply producing more goods than the existing market could absorb. How there can be theoretically an overproduction in goods which are really desirable is still a great mystery to economists; but it is not denied that there is such a thing as an effective overproduction, and that it is a common thing.

The market by September of 1929 was so flooded with goods of all kinds, or at least so threatened with the flood of goods that managed barely to be held back from production by plants capable of producing and yearning to produce them, that advertising and salesmanship became aggressive as never before in the effort to move the consumers. But this resource failed in the degree that consumers were not willfully withholding their patronage but really had not the means to buy. Schemes of purchase by installment succeeded in selling many bills of goods; but they strained the credit of houses still further; and these transactions were often going to turn out not to represent sales at all because the purchase was never going to be completed.

(2) Another kind of occupation that could not last was that of the builders—almost the most sensitive and precarious of occupations. It was a period of prodigious building. It had to be, because it was an age when fresh money out of the profits of a business whose volume had never been equaled[,] increased by credit which was readily available, was pouring into investment; and investment means fundamentally the erection of plant.[3] A boom period wears the look of feverish occupation largely because those who are not employed in the existing plant are being employed as builders of new plant. But the new plant is going to increase the existing volume of production, which is already an overproduction, and the building of the builders becomes a dangerous liability and not a

3. Ransom frequently uses "plant" and "plants" in this way—without the use of a preceding definite or indefinite article.

source of strength. If only there might have been a series of well-planned earthquakes, or cyclones, which might have destroyed the new buildings as fast as they went up! Then no harm would have been done by the attempt to make extravagant additions to productive plant, and an age of building could have continued to be an age of building. But no such thing happened. The thing that did happen was inevitable. A season later, or a few seasons later, when the new plant was put to producing in its turn, it became apparent to everybody that it had no real economic function to serve, but was excessive plant. Then the building stopped, and the personnel engaged in it was no longer in receipt of wages and in a position to patronize the producers, so that even their old rate of production was now excessive. The units began to cease operations one by one. Each stoppage of a payroll cut down the market for the other units that were still producing, and the depression gathered head like a snowball. It was in this style that late 1929 passed drearily into 1930, into 1931, and even, to the general amazement, into 1932.

(3) The third group of perishable occupations was that of employees who were going to be superseded by technology—by labor-saving machinery, and by economies in organization and processes of production. Efficiency in production is admirable in principle, and sometimes the release of laborers from an industry whose new equipment enables it to spare them permits them to go into new industries that are waiting for manpower. Unfortunately it does not lie in the nature of business ownership to wait and see that this is going to happen before turning the laborers out. And when once the crisis has come, and the boom has turned into the depression, the productive plants must redouble their efforts to keep afloat by saving costs, and to save costs by devising fresh economies at the expense of payroll. Invention and management never work so hard to cut down the labor requirement as during hard times. And this reduction is in each case permanent. Labor is forever dispossessed[4] of that much of its specific

4. The original reads "dispossed." "Disposed" seems unlikely as the intended word.

occupation, and can only live in hope that some other need for it will turn up.

———————

What then is the "normal" figure of production to which we may reasonably expect to return, and under which our productive plant, heavily reduced by that scrapping of plant which takes place through bankruptcies and forced liquidations, may expect to flourish once more? It seems reasonable to say that it will be a figure which will hardly re-engage soon all those who are now without occupation. We used to think we needed immigration to get the manpower for our promising industries. Is it possible that we need now to start emigration, in order to dispose painlessly of the superfluous citizens who have no economic function in our economic society?

———————

Humanitarians are much concerned today with relieving the unemployed, in the sense of finding money and handing it to them to live on. That is the least we can do for them at the moment. But economists are concerned with restoring them to livelihood, and making it unnecessary to resort to philanthropic drives for their relief. More employment for the unemployed, less employment for the humanitarians.

Let us conceive the economic problem of our society in its simplest sense as an occupational problem: how to find occupation for those who have none, and how to find remunerative occupation for those whose occupation has become only a formal or waiting one. The chief demand upon our statesmen at this moment, or it may be the chief demand upon our private but leading political economists[,] is to place every member of our society into some permanent economic position.

I suggest that one occupation is quite available for those of us who need it, and that, in fact, it is where we are least likely to look for it, or right under our noses.

Before naming it precisely, I should like to ask the question, From where did all these superfluous men, now squeezed out of their nominal occupations, originally come? The number of them is large, but they are the excess of workers in a plant that is huge. This plant produced in 1928, the last full year of our prosperity, something like five times as much as its nearest competitor. It had expanded to these proportions rather rapidly, and though the increase of productivity per capita through technology made much of it possible, it was obliged to make tremendous drafts upon a fresh source of manpower somewhere or other in order to operate. It recruited from several sources. There was first of all the "natural increase" in the given industrial population. But this was far behind the rate of increase which the expanding plant demanded. There was immigration, which took from the European populations on a very large scale. Even so, the immigrants who entered the American labor market were not, after a certain point, the chief source of supply, and as a matter of fact they finally ceased to be wanted. After the world war we legislated immigration nearly out of existence. Already we were feeling crowded, and the problem of occupation was presenting itself. Another accession of personnel was that made by the negro. In increasing numbers the negroes left the South and entered the industrial occupations in the East and Middle West. They made a considerable item.

But the chief source of manpower for our scheme of production was unquestionably the native American population that had been living quietly and a little bit primitively on the farms.[5] The accession made by the negroes belongs really under this head, for they came out of a country life. It was because the old-fashioned farmers of America went industrial, and migrated in an accelerating stream to the towns, that the capitalistic community was swamped beneath a personnel greater than it could assimilate solidly into its economy. That is at least the meaning of our overproduction on the side of the productive personnel. The fact is

5. Ransom did not capitalize "native" and did not mean "indigenous" or "Indian."

worth pondering when we study the grievous breakdown of occupation today. The date of the migration from the farm is of course a little indeterminate. It began when the industrial revolution first gathered head in America in the Nineteenth Century, but it evidently did not proceed very much too fast till about the late war time. Then there was a boom in production that promised to occupy profitably all the capital and all the personnel that would engage in it. It persisted even after the war. The soldiers themselves when they were demobilized looked about them as a matter of course for positions within the industrial plant. It was as if America had decided to move to town. The farm population went down faster than ever.

In theory the farmers were well within economic logic in making the move. It promised to increase their personal fortunes, and incidentally the wealth of the nation at large. Industry is more productive than old-fashioned farming. But unfortunately it sometimes proves too productive; it steps up production before it has developed the necessary market. Capitalistic society has not learned how to operate its productive plant smoothly, but is subject to dislocations and stoppages that cost the economic lives of many of its members. The old-fashioned farmers in joining this society were risking a secure if modest living for a precarious prospect of wealth, and for some of them it now definitely turns out to have been a poor gamble. There was room in the productive plant for some, but not for all that crowded suddenly into it. They might well have come in more gradually, and hoped thereby to make their tenure of industrial citizenship a little firmer.

But let bygones be bygones. The question [is], What will these unwanted industrialists, who are largely ex-farmers, do next?

———————

It is only on its present scale, of course, that the occupational problem is a new one. It used to be easy for the man whose occupation failed him to fall back upon another one which made all comers welcome and which he could reasonably count upon to support him. What was the admirable occupation which was always ready in this manner to save the economic society from its own mistakes? Nothing more nor less than agriculture; the common occupation, or the staple one, even in a society that had developed many; and by long odds the most reliable one, or the stable one.

Let us think back for a moment upon an economic era that is past, and that was quite different in its principles from the era of today. The difference was, perhaps chiefly, that the economic organization was not vast and close as it is today. The ruling unit of organization was not a whole national system of production and trade; it was the country community, largely sufficient unto itself; unless indeed it was the country household, which was organized as a little independent system going mostly if not completely on its own. That economic era was dominated by local or even household autonomy; decidedly by little business, not by big business.

Let us imagine the old-fashioned country community acting as a fairly self-contained economic unit. The bulk of its population consisted of farmers, who took their necessities from the land for immediate use. They found it too laborious, however, to practice a perfect self-sufficiency, and so they had their county town, to which they sold some of their produce, and from which in turn they bought the services necessary to complement their own labors.

(I shall make much use of the phrase *self-sufficient farmers*, but it must be conceded that never in American history since the earliest colonial days, or nowhere except out on the farthest frontier, have the farmers been quite self-sufficient. Nobody wanted them to be. In addition to feeding themselves they have always fed the industrial and professional population in the towns. Let it be assumed that every time the word *self-sufficient* occurs in this book it is to mean *nearly self-sufficient*.)

The farmers made the staples of their own living, but they made some money crops besides and sold them. They took their stuff to town and with the proceeds of sale secured their law and government, their professional needs, their tools and machine-made articles, the sugar and spices and coffee and tea and other primary products which they could not take from their own soil; and they even made exchanges with each other in the native products of the region. Some of these services had to come of course from larger towns elsewhere and from remote countries, and they implied the existence of a national and even an international economic order, which was a money-using order. But the national and international orders were fairly subordinate to the agrarian or community order, in that the main reliance of the citizens was upon their own home-made products, and in a pinch they could manage with these alone.

Suppose now that a bright farmer felt it to his taste to stop farming and set up as a merchant in the town. He would be abandoning his self-sufficiency in favor of an economy in which he must live by trade and patronage rather than by the direct fruit of his labors; he would have to become a social creature and his individual independence would be gone. But at least the town was not entirely foreign to him; it was only a country town in the midst of a farming county. It had no Chamber of Commerce asking the farmers to crowd into it to live, and hoping that a national economy would send a factory to the spot to give them some occupation. But it let him come in if he liked, and in coming he was not throwing himself upon the mercies of a great impersonal society, but a small homely one in which he could see precisely what he was doing. Nevertheless, the town might not really need another merchant; in which case he would struggle for a time, doing damage meanwhile to the other merchants, but eventually might have to admit defeat and give up his business. Where would he go? There is no doubt that the community would expect him, and if necessary assist him, to go back to farming; and the land, when the prodigal returned to it, would be as kind as if he had never left it. So far as America is concerned, there always was land enough for him to till. There was no such problem as overpopulation. The sons of the landed aristocrats, who were sometimes numerous, might not inherit as much land as they wanted, and some of them were rather expected to go into business and the professions. But when they failed, they could always return to the land in some sort of capacity; they could go to the frontier and take up large areas of free or cheap land if they felt so ambitious; but it was not necessary to feel too sorry for them if they went home into a humbler status. Many professional men played both ends of the economic game, and did not know whether they were professional men and retainers of society or independent planters. The commonest kind of intuition, reinforced by the voice of tradition, told them they had better not get too far from the land. It was a landed community.

The country towns of an older generation—the English used to refer to them very accurately as "market" towns—have changed beyond knowing, which is to say that they have about vanished from the American scene, as an incident of the great economic "advance." The farmer who would now go to town to start in business does not set up his own store so often as he accepts employment with a national chain, or a big concern whose business is national though its plant may be situated in the town. Big business has succeeded little business, and the town is caught up into the cycle of the national economy, prospering as it prospers and going down when it has a depression. The marks of this deterioration are written all over the face of the town, and registered in the atmosphere which one feels in the town, but I shall not stop to record them. The town scarcely has any control over its own economic life. It is only an outpost of empire. No farmer moving to town today therefore is making himself a member of a small, autonomous, shock-proof society. He will fail in business when every one else is failing, and the day when the failures came one at a time and could be absorbed by the community has gone, apparently forever. Let us not take the time to mourn for the lost town.

But the land is with us still, as patient and nearly as capable as ever. Which brings us to the query: Why is not the land perfectly available today for its ancient use as a refuge individually for those who have failed in the business economy, when that refuge is needed as never before?

———————

It is still available. That is the answer, but it is so simple that nobody is prepared to believe it. We no longer think kindly of the land when we think as economists, and we would prefer to look almost anywhere else for our economic salvation. That is because we have seen the landed life in our time degraded and its incomparable economic advantage disused and almost forgotten. There is just one thing that town men know for certain about the contemporary farmer: that he is in the most unpaid occupation in our whole society. The farm owners stagger under mortgages, and often produce crops in spite of the fact that the prices they receive will not pay the cost of production. Their employees are lower than the robots of the cheapest factories in the wage scale, lower than the women in the sweatshops. But behind this condition is a piece of ruinous economic folly.

The American farmers in "going productive" did a thorough job of it; they went in more senses than one. Some of them, as we have seen, made a clean break with the land and went into the factories and offices of the towns. But even those who stayed at home ceased to farm in the old self-sufficient way, by which they had made a living first and a money crop second; now they began to devote themselves exclusively to their money crops, expecting to take the money and buy themselves a better living out of the stores than they could have made with their own hands. Think of farmers buying hams and bacon, butter and milk and eggs, jams and pickles and preserves, and labor to whitewash their fences, prop up their porches, and prettify their lawns! Townspeople have always bought of such things, but it is a novelty for farmers. Nothing less than an economic revolution swept over the American farms. It consisted in the substitution of the capitalistic or money economy for the self-sufficient or agrarian economy. The change, like the migration to town, required a period rather than a single date; it was under way when the war began, and it was virtually complete when the world settled down to peace.

The capitalistic or money economy is "efficient" on the farm, almost as much as in the factory. It implies specialization of function rather than the completeness and independence of the individual; each function contributing to the whole and taking its remuneration in money. When applied to farming, it assigns to each piece of land its special use, equips the farmer with the best tools to work it regardless of expense, and expects him to devote himself with perfect concentration to obtaining maximum output in the specified product. If a nation is rather short in its supply of land, capitalistic farming will make the most of what there is, and the old-fashioned agrarian farming cannot be tolerated because it is wasteful. The old farmer, whose object was to supply himself before he catered to a market, was a sort of Jack-at-all-trades, like some strange producer who had elected to run a one-man factory and consume its production himself. That is not the scientific or modern theory of business, which is essentially big business, and is based on the willingness of everybody to forgo producing his own living and to produce something strictly for sale, even at the risk of disaster when his particular product cannot be sold. The difference in efficiency between the two economies of the land is such that the following is scarcely an exaggeration of facts already made manifest: the same land might support a million self-sufficient farmers, or it might support a working society of twice the number if farmed properly for money, and yet require only five hundred thousand of them to live and work on the land, leaving the other million and a half to perform the more industrial functions in the towns; and the latter society would be not only richer in the aggregate but richer in per capita wealth. That is a familiar type of argument, and lies either as an intuition or as an open theory behind our whole capitalistic development.

But it would be miraculous if every new member of the capitalistic society should fly unerringly to his proper station and live and function and prosper there forever. Many mistakes must be made in assigning the occupations in so intricate and large a society, and a great many people must get hurt. The ex-farmers who went to town know all about that. But what happens now to the farm population that is left, reduced though it may be, when it repudiates the old way of farming for independence and security and applies the money economy rigorously, and finally, to the land itself?

Farming exhibits now a greater percentage of failures, or a greater excess of personnel, than any other large American occupation. Farmers are not able to go to the stores with money jingling in their pockets to buy freely of the comforts and decencies of life. Their houses are falling down in a manner which would have mortified their grandfathers, because with all their money-cropping they have not made the money to hire the carpenter and the painter. They set their tables in a style quite unworthy of the tradition of farmer's plenty. They worry themselves to death over their unhappy relations with the bank or the loan company that holds the mortgage, the hardware firm that equipped the farm with its modern machinery. And all this was true in 1928 as well as in 1931. Ever since the farmers became money-makers they have had nothing but unsuccess. We were reading about the farmer's sufferings long before the papers began to fill up with news about a depression for everybody. The farmers have complained of their situation, naturally, and there is plenty of sympathy for them, or was before we all had troubles of our own. But every reform movement which they advocate, or which their political patrons advocate for them, seems to be only another artificial and privileged way to make more money than they can possibly make under the natural operation of economic law.

There is a simple reason why farming as money-making cannot flourish in America, either now or soon. There is too much land for that, and too many farmers on the land. When it produces it overproduces. The total productive capacity of land and personnel under these circumstances is certainly two or three times greater than its market. Money-making, so far as the American farmers are concerned, is like the grace of God: it cannot be pursued successfully as an end in itself.

The capitalistic doctrine, nevertheless, swept all before it in this country, including at last the farmers. It was perhaps not so strange if farmers grew envious of the quick wealth it created, tired of their home-made security, and trekked in ever larger numbers to the city; or even if, where they stayed on the farm, they applied to it at last the capitalistic technique and farmed it exclusively for money. But it was also not strange if, when they had made a capital instrument out of their land, they found it so unprofitable that their migration cityward was accelerated; economic compulsion was behind that. Almost any other occupation looked better than farming to the amateur capitalistic economist.

At this moment, however, an alteration has come over the economic landscape. The money-making farmers, who are making no money, are looking as usual at the other occupations to see if there is no room for them there, while the other occupations are looking back at the farmer and wondering if there is really no chance on the farm, with neither party finding the slightest ground for encouragement. There is no migration from the farm to the city because the city has no more occupation to spare. And there is a little enough migration in the opposite sense; yet there is a little. Some eccentric persons move to the country to escape from an overcompetitive society and make a primitive living in comparative peace; the Thoreaus of our time. More important than that, proposals are heard now and again in America for the relief of some local unemployment by colonizing the unemployed on the nearest unoccupied land; precisely the thing which the Austrian government is said to be doing, and some of the unemployment committees in the German municipalities, though land is scarce in Germany.

In just such a movement as this lies, I think, our readiest and surest deliverance provided we will conceive it on a large scale and work it hard. We shall not be making much use of it so long as we think of it as a makeshift measure which for the time being will furnish the needy with some wretched and uncomfortable kind of subsistence that is better than starvation. I am afraid it is felt that a man reduced to raising his own potatoes and chickens has about the rating of the cow turned into the pasture; but we might question this feeling when we consider the generations of men who, till quite recently in the world's history, lived in what they often regarded as comfort and dignity on the soil without the use of a great deal of money for purchasing goods upon the market. I cannot imagine why a serious application of the old economy to the farm today would not produce at least as much comfort and dignity as it ever did.

We have unsuccessful men of business today, but we have always had them. We have more of them, for reasons that are not subject to their determination, but that does not matter. Such men used to go back and be reabsorbed in the landed occupation they had come from. It is precisely what they should do today. It is hard to say why they do not, in numbers sufficient to constitute a movement, except that they, and we who might be helping them, now understand the landed occupation in an improper sense. But that misunderstanding, though it is general, can be remedied.

I venture to suggest to the patriots and economists that they try to re-establish self-sufficiency as the proper economy for the American farm, and thus save the present farmers; and at the same time that they try to get back into this economy as many as possible of the derelicts of the capitalistic economy who are now stranded in the city. I suggest an agrarian agitation, sponsored by people who may speak with authority, and leading to action on the part of people who are on the land now and people who may return there.

I shall not now go into any detail about the conditions and method of such a movement. But I remark that the new agrarian farmers will be the most innocent and esteemed members in the economic society because they alone will not injure each other through competition. If there is land for all, they cut nobody's throat by farming it in this manner; and there is land for all. Any man today who temperamentally cannot bear to hurt his needy neighbor had better take to the agrarian way of living, and any political economist who deplores the inevitable inhumanity of the competitive scramble might well approve a movement which is capable of enlisting an indefinite fraction of the crowded capitalistic society and planting it in an economy which is not mainly competitive. By agrarianism we may restore to our economic life some of the humanity which it lacks today.

———————

This is an occupational prescription for an occupational problem. The difficulty in the way of taking it is mainly an impediment in our habit of economic thought: we have subscribed too heartily to the doctrine of the higher productivity of the capitalistic economy.

But here is a very broad consideration which has to do with America and economic destiny. Is there no relation between the economic life of these States and their peculiar natural resources? We have a large population, but an area more than large enough for it, and well blessed in soil and climate. The acreage in fact is excessive if we intend to put it to work producing foodstuffs and raw materials scientifically and capitalistically like a factory; on that basis the country population which tends it is overproductive and the victim of insufficient occupation in the strictest economic sense. But nothing could be more absurd to the bird's-eye view of some old-fashioned economic realist than the phenomenon of men actually sitting down to unemployment in the country; though he might expect some unemployment in our cities, which have grown like mushrooms.

A foreigner touring for some thousands of miles through America remarked that he was struck by the contrast between the unkempt, neglected, uninhabited aspect of our countryside and the state of swarming congestion in our cities. That remark was made in the middle 20's; what would he say today, now that so many thousands of the city multitudes are jobless men walking the streets, and sometimes making "demonstrations," while the country-side is more vacant and untidy than ever? What, after all, is our land thought to be good for? Is the bulk of it only for picnics and camping parties, is it for scenery? Is it for the entertainment of the Boy Scouts? It used to be thought good for homes. Unfit for intensive money-making, because of its very excellence and abundance, it is ideal for home-making. That happens to be the very thought which inspired the fathers to found the colonies, then the Union, then one by one the successive new States. It is remarkable that an admirable and obvious thought like that should ever have slipped out of our notice, but it will be as good as ever if we will entertain it again. There is nothing the matter with it.

Perhaps we shall like it better when we set it beside the thought that not all the nations have such a brilliant opportunity as we do. In Britain, for example, they cannot afford agrarianism, they have not the land to provide homes for all that need them; and I, and most people, are sorry. In America we may realize an economic destiny much kinder and more secure than has generally been allotted to the peoples of this earth.

Chapter 2

THE EXCESS OF CAPITAL

We may or may not be proud of our material civilization. But it is perfectly in order for us all to repeat in unison, even if we have to be led by the Secretaries of the Chambers of Commerce, "It is private capitalism that has made us what we are today."

For how does this material civilization touch us personally? It defines for us usually our occupations, which in these days have a rare degree of specialization or distinctitude; it keeps us, rather punctiliously for the most part, in money; and when we take our money and go to market, it gives us access to goods of the greatest variety and ingenuity. But all these benefits are continuing functions that are tied up inseparably with the operation of large capitalistic enterprises. Not the job nor the money nor the commodity would be there ready for us in its present form if some private persons had not acquired much capital and with it set great producing plants to going, and to distributing their benefits according to the firm but lavish formula of capitalism. The comprehensive magic of capital!

It is easy and often harmless to rhapsodize about capital, as if it had a soul, as if capital were Capital. Some talk about it as a greedy monster devouring his innocent victims, who are the laborers, the poor. It is commoner in our neighborhood of the world to praise it as a beneficent spirit that never wearies of well-doing;

31

we hear that capital "wants to improve our human life, wants nothing for itself but the chance to keep employed in the public interest." But such talk is poetry and fiction rather than economics. It does more credit to the imagination than to the realistic intelligence. Capital is simply an inert material possession that works in the hands of the capitalist, and the soul of the thing, if any, belongs to the capitalist too. We shall not develop the entire truth about capital if we talk about it in these interesting but animistic terms.

So let us not grow mystical about the loving or diabolical nature of capital, seeing there is really no such thing, and ask rather, What is the motive of the man with capital? The answer to this question is certain and fairly simple. The man with capital has got beyond that low economic stage where he is looking for subsistence. His motive is, specifically, the acquisition of more capital; incidentally, or fundamentally, the projection of his ego into larger channels of wealth, influence, and power. Nobody in his senses, I think, will find anything monstrous or iniquitous in that motive; it is precisely the motive which we impute to him every day when we go to have business dealings with him. His professional status and his professional aim in our society are very well understood. He wants to make his capital earn money which he can turn into more capital; to make a big capital out of a little capital, and a bigger capital out of a big capital. Therefore with his capital he undertakes to found his ingenious technical producing establishment, to employ workmen at an honest wage, and to market products which are desirable and cheap; because that is the way in which he can best make his capital earn.

The capitalists, who are relatively few, employ the wage-earners, who are many. Is it fair? Mr. and Mrs. Webb, contemporary and English, but deriving as economists from the great Marx, have brought forward a typical indictment of capitalism, and perhaps this is its chief count: "The separation of the workers from the ownership of the instruments of production rather than the series of technological discoveries that transformed industrial processes is, to the scientific economist, as well as to the Socialist, the essential feature of the Industrial Revolution."[1] That is to say, capitalism has performed wonderful feats in the production of useful commodities, which is good; but it has conferred the ownership and direction of the producing tools upon a comparative few, which is bad. But just how bad is a matter of dispute. And the fact remains that the thing which is bad has been the precise means of obtaining the thing which is good. Without private ownership of capital, no technique, no large-scale production. Without the development of the modern relation of owners to employees, the benefits of modern material civilization would not be here for us to enjoy.

The private capitalist is therefore important in our economic society far beyond the general run of persons; he moulds the forms of our economic life. Most of us have only to consent to his brilliant dispositions and do as he tells us. But the consensus of opinion is that on the whole we have found it rather good for us; evidently he has known what was best. And just here is something really wonderful. The men with the capital, whose motives are wholly private, have put it to work in a manner that was good for everybody concerned. Private capitalism has produced public benefit. The aggregate of all the private transactions is a system that a political economist can approve.

A political economist is a person who is scheming not for his own good or the good of somebody else but only for the good of all. He is the statesman, or the technical advisor of the statesman. The happiest discovery he can possibly make is that there is no special need for a political economy of the spectacular or heroic sort; of one that would require the state to make and enforce some very difficult economic disposition of its citizens. He discovers, in the present instance, that there is no necessary conflict between private good and the good of all when capitalism is running the show. The capitalist wants to make his money earn, the rest of us want

1. Sidney and Beatrice (Potter) Webb (1859–1947; 1858–1943), British social scientists, members of the Fabian Society, and founding members of the London School of Economics. Supporters of the Soviet Union, their books include *The History of Trade Unionism* (1894) and *Industrial Democracy* (1897).

to make our labor earn, but both can succeed through a single identical enterprise of which, as it happens, the capitalist has the exclusive direction. The great producer wants to sell, the rest of us want to buy, but the harder he tries to sell the easier he makes it for us to buy. More than a century ago, when the Industrial Revolution was young, the political economists saw precisely how the land lay and gave their endorsement to capitalism. The shrewd advice which they offered to the state was: *Laissez faire*; let things alone; let the capitalist and the non-capitalist make all the trades they please, even if it is invariably the capitalist who takes the initiative and draws up the contract. The admonition was heeded. It made life easy for the statesman, and in the course of time it has brought about the prosperity we have today.

The success of the scheme rested on the remarkable fact that people without any particular coercion, and for perfectly private reasons, would adapt themselves helpfully to each other's economic existence. The natural or private action turned out to be the rational or social action. And to what was this blessed coincidence due, how was it possible? In the long run I imagine we had just as well be content to say simply that it was due to the Providence who gave to the world such a modicum of rationality as it has; that it was the provision of a kind Nature determined that her frail creatures should realize an effective economic society without heroics and with very little fuss.

Which is all very pretty. It is as pretty as I know how to make it, using the perfectly orthodox account of the glories of our capitalistic accomplishments. Nevertheless there have been some frictions, some knocks and uproars, in the development of our capitalistic establishment, whose progress has not exactly been a monotonous march of triumph. People have rallied against capitalism many times. What is more to the point, there is at that moment a tremendous revulsion against capitalism which is taking definite action in some parts of Europe, threatening action in other parts, and talking in a most disrespectful manner even in America. Heroics have arrived. For our capitalism today is not giving quite the satisfaction we have been instructed to expect. The degree of satisfaction varies widely with the individual, and for some it is the profoundest dissatisfaction. The capitalists have made mistakes to the grievous hurt of the non-capitalists and, strangely enough, to their own hurt. Many people therefore are reviewing the history and theory of capitalism to see if it can really be the basis of a political economy.

———————

It is tempting to personify capital after all, though I shall not be sentimental about it, but only invest it with one simple behavior-pattern which it exhibits over and over though with all its boundless animal energy. Evidently capital longs solely to earn income, and finds a thousand handsome ways to gratify this longing. Let us say that income is the child, whose destiny is to become itself a grown-up capital, earning income in its turn. The basic and incessant impulse of capital is reproduction.

The fateful thing about this impulse is a property which capital shares with guinea pigs and tame rabbits: it breeds fast. It knows no technique of birth control. It breeds and breeds until, periodically, there has come definitely too much capital into existence. The business depressions, of which we are enjoying the latest and perhaps the finest example, are complexes of economic phenomena, but the basic phenomenon may well be the overcapitalization of industry. Let us not abuse capital for being only what its nature requires it to be. Its motive is simple and not at all malicious. Instead of inveighing against the "excesses" of capital— meaning its reputed tyranny, greed, extortion, oppression—it seems much more to the point to cite simply its sheer excess; there is too much of it.

A sum of money put out at 4 per cent compound interest will in a little more than two centuries grow to 250,000 per cent of itself. Or, 1 per cent of the total annual income of the United States, at that rate and in that period, would amount to far more than the present wealth of the world. However, that is only a paper calculation; it will not really happen, as we all know. No banks are powerful enough to guarantee 4 per cent compounded annually on an account that is going to increase indefinitely, no sound bank will continue an account that has grown out of all proportion to the bank's facilities for placing loans. The banks that keep this money will have to put it out in productive industry somewhere to get a return on it and pay the interest; but there will be time after time, like the present time, when there is small chance of getting a return on large new capital investment. You are only freeing your assets, or perhaps you are even throwing them away, when you pour them into an industrial world already overcapitalized and over-productive.

And yet a savings of 1 per cent of income is far below the usual thing—it was many times this figure in the great days preceding the crash of 1929. And a 4 per cent expectation means a decidedly modest sort of investment. No one would look twice at a person who only saved and invested on that pusillanimous scale.

A capitalist, defined for our purpose, is a man whose income is derived from interest, or from the profits of investment, rather than from wages. But the trouble is that the capitalist, by re-investing a part of this income, expects to draw interest on interest and profit on profit. In so far as he succeeds, his capital accumu-lates, and the combined accumulation of all the thrifty capitalists soon amounts to an excessive capitalization of all the industries in sight, with a great deal of loose money looking anxiously for some fresh industries that might yet be capitalized and set going.

Unfortunately, there is a sort of Malthusian principle which applies to capital more clearly than we have ever seen it applying to population. Capital tends to increase faster than its means of subsistence; its means of subsistence being its power to draw in-terest. Eventually there is so much capital on hand that a fierce competition ensues in which a great deal of capital is destined to perish. The business cycle may well be regarded as the conse-quence of the proclivities of capital for rapid breeding. In this cycle we may perhaps distinguish three general stages: (1) Large income from capital and large fresh capitalization out of income; (2) a defi-nite overcapitalization, overproduction, stagnation of business; (3) shrinkage of capital through bankruptcy and liquidation, and a reorganization that amounts to a decapitalization.

The net result is that we must write off as pure waste much or all of that income which has produced the overcapitalization, lain like an incubus upon business, and then been wiped out as the condition to a fresh start. This income might originally have been spent, but unfortunately it was saved; and it might have been saved in a stocking, or under a hearthstone, but unfortunately it was invested; it was put precisely where it would do the most harm. The capitalist who proceeded quite frankly to spend his large income upon the luxuries appropriate to his station would be regarded as a monster of selfishness, and he would enrage the people with his superior privileges. He might indeed hasten the war of the classes, to which the Marxians have sometimes looked forward pleasantly, and that is not his cue at all. Mr. J. M. Keynes in his *Economic Consequences of the Peace*[2] has a famous passage in which, after reviewing the part which savings and investment played in developing the modern wealth of Europe, he tells how the capitalists won public consent for their procedure:

> Thus this remarkable system depended for its growth on a double bluff or deception. On the one hand the laboring classes accepted from ignorance or powerlessness, or were compelled, persuaded, and cajoled by custom, convention, authority, and the well-established order of society into accepting, a situation in which they could call their own very little of the cake that they and nature and the capitalists were co-operating to produce. And on the other hand the capitalist classes were allowed to call the best part of the cake theirs and were theoretically free to consume it, on the tacit underlying condition that they consumed very little of it in practice. The duty of "saving" became nine-tenths of virtue, and the growth of the cake the object of true religion. There grew round the non-consumption of the cake all those instincts of puritanism which in other ages has withdrawn itself from the world and has neglected the arts of production as well as those of enjoyment. And so the cake increased; but to what end was not clearly contemplated.[3]

2. John Maynard Keynes, *Economic Consequences of the Peace* (New York: Harcourt, Brace, and Howe, 1920).

3. *The Collected Writings of John Maynard Keynes* (London: Macmillan, 1919), 2:11–12.

The American capitalists have followed the same general procedure. They have increased their capital by adding to it its own income, instead of spending that income. They have been very little concerned with the fear that it was being increased faster than it could sustain itself. But we can see today that the 100 per cent patriot capitalists who recently were so intent on "not selling America short" and boasted of "putting the money back into the business" were leading American industry into a trap from which it will not come out with all that it took in.

Overcapitalization consists in a capital plant whose production is an overproduction. The two terms refer to the same thing. An industry is overcapitalized when it is capable of producing more goods than it can sell; and it is overproductive, according to the usage of most economists, not necessarily when it is actually producing and sending to market more goods than it can sell, but when it has a normal plant capacity or expectation of producing goods in volume more than the market will take.

But it is commonly said by economists that we do not even today have a "real" overproduction in America, and that the trouble is not so much an overproduction as an underconsumption. The moral of this position is probably a bad one; that we are not to discourage at all the production of articles useful to mankind nor limit the capital plant behind this production, while we go to work developing the consumers in some manner to the point where their purchasing power is equal to appropriating the good things which they are offered. It is argued that as long as there are hungry people in China, in India, in New York City and in drought-stricken Arkansas, there cannot be an overproduction on the farms; as long as there are people in the world needing cars to ride in, there is no overproduction in the automobile industry; and so on through all the list of commodities.

At first sight this use of terms does not seem to make for economic reasoning, but to come from persons who do not know what "real" means, and are not realists. The overproduction is real in an economic sense which governs the producers, though it may not be real in some distant and celestial sense which might govern the angels. The actual economic system rests on a basis of free exchange. If we offer our services without receiving a consideration in return, we have engaged in philanthropy but not in business. The role is noble but not economic. Our producing machinery may now have, or with encouragement it might soon have, a capacity sufficient to feed and clothe and maintain in comfort the whole of our population. But this machinery is capital, and it was set up with a definite motive: to get money for its products. It would not otherwise have been set up, and it cannot otherwise continue to work. It secures as good an earning as it can, and it will operate even if its earning is very low, but beyond that its operation is suicide. Who will pay capital to operate at a loss? Overproduction consists practically in producing, not more goods than can be given away, but more goods than can be sold.

But this argument is only by way of skirmish; it does not capture a quite extensive and deeply-trenched position which is held by some quite orthodox modern economists. Let us examine the ground from a fresh angle.

Economic theory can scarcely say why there should ever be overproduction in goods that are really desired. Suppose we do a little double-entry book-keeping, and regarded all the money assets of an industry for a moment as also liabilities. The result is illuminating. The assets are the revenues that flow into it from the sales of its products; what becomes of them? Money is the power to purchase, its nature is to circulate; it comes in on the side of receipts, to lie in the pockets of the owners, managers, workmen, distributors, salesmen, to all that we will bring under the personnel of this industry as having a share in production; but it does not expect to lie there long, for as a liability it is going to be spent on the products of the other industries. The cost of any set of products, when it is realized and returned to the producers, becomes a purchasing power, a patronage to be distributed among producers in general. Production therefore necessarily generates its equivalent in consumption, and pays its own way. How could it fail? According to this logic, $P = C$; production automatically creates and balances consumption.

It does not matter in the least how the revenues of an industry are shared among its personnel, though it might seem to matter. It does not even matter—for logic—how hoggish or profiteering the owners are in seeking high prices for their product, nor how they stint their employees in their scale of wages.

Suppose the owners are able to reserve out of their gross revenues a handsome 15 per cent for themselves as capital earnings, after paying out 85 per cent to all those who have contributed their services to production; and suppose they find 5 per cent sufficient for their living expenses and 10 per cent remaining for disposal. They would not be capitalists if they did not see in the 10 per cent a pretty addition to their capital. With the least possible delay they put it back into the capital plant. They do not spend it in the sense in which the employees spend wages. And there it might seem to the uninitiated economist that he had stumbled upon a glaring violation of the law of double-entry book-keeping upon which the life of trade depends. It is indeed a critical situation, sometimes a fatal one; but the trouble is not so obvious as might seem. It looks as if the owners of this business have failed in their obligation by holding back 10 per cent of their revenues from the general purchase fund, so that when P, the value of their product, is 100, C, the consumption-power which the transaction liberates, is only 90, and P is not balanced with C. But the theory is that $P = C$ automatically, and that greedy or ambitious owners cannot help it; and the theory is not so easily upset as this.

We have only to look closely at the actual disposition of the owners' 10 per cent. It is true they do not spend it on cars, radios, clothing, and the like as the other 90 per cent has been spent; they put it back into the business. But in order to put it back into the business they must spend it, and it goes back into circulation one way as well as the other. The fact is that they pay it out to the builders who are employed to erect the new addition to plant. The builders then spend the 10 per cent, only a little behind schedule as compared with the personnel inside the plant who have already spent their 90 per cent. In the end the whole income of the business becomes outgo, though there has been a delay for some of it.

Next year the volume of production from the enlarged plant will be 10 per cent greater than this year. But the same economic reasoning will apply to it no matter what its volume. Its P will be balanced in the same way by its C. Perhaps the owners will be able to save out another 10 per cent of the revenues for the reinvestment; their principal difficulty in doing so will lie in satisfying those who contribute to production with their remuneration of 90 per cent of gross income. If the owners are able year after year to add 10 per cent of income to their capital, it will increase by regular geometrical progression, and in any subsequent year will have increased $(1.10)^{n-1}$ times, when n is the number of years completed on this basis.

But suppose all the plants in all the industries in the nation are expanding at this rate. Or suppose, to be more conservative, they are all expanding at the rate of 4 per cent each year, just as the money in an ordinary savings bank account appreciates at that rate. The capital wealth of the nation after n years will be the original wealth multiplied by $(1.04)^{n-1}$, which is 2 when n is 18, 4 when n is 35, 16 when n is 70, but 2,500 after the lapse of a couple of centuries. Economic theory on its mathematical side offers every encouragement for the view that the wealth of a country will increase 2,500 times if 4 per cent of income is religiously put back into productive capital; such being the singular virtue of compound interest. But we do not hope for it; we hardly dared hope for it even in the year 1928. Our skepticism is not due to any lack of confidence in our political stability as a nation. But we doubt, in the first place, if it is possible by any mechanical ingenuity to increase our productivity to that extent; and in the second place, if our economic system will be stable enough to consolidate all the gains to which our mechanical genius entitles us, and will not break down time and again within the period and lose valuable ground.

The growth of capital, whether it has the regularity of geometrical progression or not, cannot take place at all without raising the issue of the supply of labor to operate the plant and make it productive. If we assume that the growth is not accompanied by any particular advances in the technique of production, then there must be a corresponding growth in the working population; the plant cannot be enlarged if no fresh workmen are available. Where do they come from? Some are the natural increase of the existing population; some are immigrants. The immigrants may be coming very rapidly, so that our plants may safely expand in order to absorb them, and then the national wealth will appreciate duly. But it will be only the aggregate national wealth that does so, not the per capita wealth. Our capitalists will be able to look forward to bigger businesses but not better ones, and our patriots will have a bigger and more powerful country behind them but not one whose citizens are more prosperous. And when finally no more fresh workmen are available, and all the old workmen have steady employment, expansion will be at an end. The last construction job for the builders will be the construction of plant which they themselves next year are to operate; their career as builders is over and henceforth they are to be inside workmen. They ought to be, at any rate; though it is entirely possible that the owners, habituated to their investment psychology, will still demand the right to earn 4 per cent with their capital, engage the builders with it as usual, and put up more plant. If they persist in this policy for 25 years, there will be as much unused plant as used plant in existence, and 96 per cent of the unused plant will be an irreclaimable waste and could not be used at all, while 4 per cent of it will be an actual waste, but could profitably be operated by the builders if the owners would let them. The inside workers will still be able to sustain the builders, as they have always done, but the builders ought to be sustaining themselves.

But far more significant is the investment not in units which duplicate old plant but in improvements to the old plant or in the substitution of new kind of plant altogether which promises a larger volume of production. It may be the same industry and the same personnel, but it will have mechanical equipment that makes the personnel more productive—not by 4 but by 6 or 10 or 50 per cent. That is the kind of capital increase that has done more than make us a wealthy nation in the aggregate, which indeed would be nothing remarkable, seeing that we are a numerous people with plenty of land and natural resources who would have a great wealth under almost any economy; but that has made us the leading nation in per capita wealth. The American workman simply turns off more production than any other, and his superiority is not due so much to himself as to the initiative of the American capitalist, who devotes his earnings faithfully to the devisal and then to the installation of superior tools and processes. The time is past when new capital plant requires a brand-new supply of labor in our economic society. Many of the new capital investments simply reach back and increase the productivity of the labor already under employment, and their total effect has been rather to bring about a superfluity of American labor than to open new markets in America for labor. The question which disturbs our economists now is not how to find manpower for the new industries but how to find employment for all the population. Technology has resulted in unemployment.

But this too is almost incomprehensible under the pure logic of economic theory. Why do not the existing industries simply absorb the extra workmen proportionately, why is not their expansion perfectly elastic and able to take care of any numbers of personnel that want to enter them? It would not seem to matter how productive these industries are; or rather, the more productive they are the better, for the greater the volume of products there will be for general distribution according to the give and take of trade. Why are our industries operating at 60 or 70 per cent capacity while the workmen who might enable them to operate at full speed are walking the streets looking for employment?

This is a mystery to which many solutions have been offered, with little agreement upon any of them. Evidently the accelerated speed of the industrial revolution of late years in America has not made the motion smoother, but more jumpy and unruly. But until a precise analysis can be made I shall repeat the word *overcapitalization* as the chief name of our economic error. It is true that it is a crude formula, and requires a great deal of qualification. It is also a provisional one, waiting on the perfect understanding of our economic processes—which may never come. Admitting that capitalists are justified by a very fine and orthodox theory in expanding their capital plant, both by way of plain addition and by way of improved equipment; admitting that it is always possible to put the blame somewhere else when the expansion causes dislocations of trade and then the general breakdown of business—nevertheless it is in this act that we can detect the nearest efficient cause of our trouble. The trouble would be avoided if the capitalists could abstain from their usual rapid expansion, let well enough alone, and sacrifice capital spread for the sake of stability. Not knowing at all how to run the present economic system in its present high-powered state, it might be well if we, or rather the capitalists, could run it in the lower gears for a while. But I am prepared for the event that this may not prove possible; the machine may not be that sort of machine. We are parts of the machine, the capitalists themselves are only parts of it, though more important ones, and we and they may find that, try as we will, we have little effect upon its motion, and will have to go out of it and build another machine that is new from the ground up before we shall have one that we can manage. I use the word overcapitalization for the sake of analysis.

It cannot be contended literally, of course, that P, the production, will automatically and without fail generate C, the consumption power to balance it. The equation is not self-working or fool-proof at all, it only defines an ideal or theoretical relation and bears on its face a logic which would encourage us to think it may not be unattainable. There is a very important consideration of fact about which it is silent. It is true that the money which comes in to pay for production goes out again to take part in consumption; *but this money must first come in.* The producer must actually sell his product. Business difficulties after all spring from that one source: failure to sell the goods which we have gone into business to produce. We have already produced the goods, or we have already set up our expensive plant to produce them, before we discover that they cannot be sold. It is an embarrassing discovery; sometimes it is fatal. When there comes to be a great glut of goods of all kinds on the market, or, what is identical in meaning, and aggregate of plant whose goods would cause a great glut if the plant dared to operate at normal, then businesses must go to failing, and a depression is imminent.

––––––––––

The consumers may fail to buy the goods offered for either of two reasons: because they have not the means; or because they do not want the goods. Most of this discussion is about the first of these events, which at the moment is the more puzzling, but it may be worth while to examine the other briefly. The producer must sell on a market where people are free to buy or not to buy. If he tries to sell them gold bricks or wooden nutmegs, or something that is honest but fantastic, or simply something that is not as good as his competitor's article, his sales will not be made, or they will decline to the point where he cannot meet the cost of production and must close down his plant. By withholding their patronage, consumers can cause any business to break.

Before the modern terms production and consumption were heard of, there was a pair of terms in use which was beautifully expressive of the human factor in the transaction: supply and demand. Consumption sounds mechanical and manageable, but demand implies the uncertainties of human choice. No one would venture to assert that supply automatically creates demand, no one would theorize to the effect that $S = D$. Economists who tend to justify the capitalistic system by abstract considerations of production and consumption might do well to revert occasionally to such simple yet concrete and mysterious terms as supply and demand.

Manufacturers today in nearly all lines of production, but especially of finished production, have to consult consumers' taste by offering goods over a range of models and prices that is far from economical. Consumers fall within many brackets of income, and the manufacturer must remember that and try for those of each bracket. General Motors offer half a dozen grades of automobile in order to fit each pocketbook in the car-purchasing class; though the Ford Motor Company may be content with two grades, hoping that a good cheap car will do for most drivers and a fine expensive care will suit the rest. It is the same way with manufacturers of radio sets, refrigerators, rugs, stationary, house fittings, chinaware, hardware, stockings, shoes, underwear, roofing, sporting goods, blankets, drygoods, canned goods, furniture, cigars, wall paper, playing cards. But there are also many kinds of taste on the part of consumers even within the same income bracket, and many possible varieties in an article of a given grade. It is hardly the tendency of the enterprising manufacturers to agree on some standard article there; each will prefer to put out his own article and to give it boldness and distinction; and then perhaps each, for fear he will not convert the public to this own taste, will put out articles resembling those of his competitors. Competitive salesmanship develops both these tendencies at once. There is also the usual necessity of changing the styles and models with each season for the fastidious customer. The manufacturer who succeeds under these conditions has to be smart, and any other kind of manufacturer is overcapitalizing as soon as he sets up in business. Business is not conducted these days by routine.

But it is not looking under the surface to see in this situation only a consumer who tyrannies over the producer, drives him to trouble and expense, and puts his business in continual hazard. It is not the consumer who really does this but the competitor. Such pains for the sake of pleasing customers mean competition, and competition means that already there is too much productive plant flooding the market with its output. Too many concerns want to share in the given trade. Some of them will hold on only so long and then go under, the casualties of that wasteful sort of enterprise which is overcapitalization. And all of them, in the meantime, will have been bearing the expense of their unsold goods, waiting till the cost may be recouped from the consumers when trade recovers, and straining their credit.

The factor of consumers' taste, after all, resolves itself into a matter of consumers' means. It is when consumption-fund is small, and too many producers have to bid for it, that they offer bargains which they cannot afford, and flatter the preferences of their customers.

———————

Let us picture the whole industrial population reduced proportionately all round and concentrated in one small town. The inhabitants are the producing personnel through the week, working in factories that encircle the town, and the consuming personnel on Saturday evenings when they bring their money to market. There is a central square on the four sides of which are the shops exhibiting their wares; they are supplied by a belt line in the rear operated by jobbers, who receive, assort, and distribute among them each week the output of the factories. Each consumer walks about the square selecting the articles that appeal to him within his price range. But the remarkable fact is, not that some inferior articles remain unsold in the shops at closing time, but that there remain unsold stocks of articles of every sort, even when the consumers have spent all their money. There is not a factory in the town that can rely on them to consume its total production. And after a time some of the more unfortunate or more inefficient factories have to discontinue for lack of patronage. But this throws a number of workers into unemployment, and the failure of their patronage is quickly felt by the other factories; some of these have to close too, or reduce their operations. Soon the whole town is suffering, in spite of its perfect modern equipment for wealth; overproduction and stoppage of income for the citizens as producers, underconsumption and want for them as consumers.

But for the fact that all the factories, and not only some, are overproductive in this exhibit, it would be easy to understand overcapitalization. It occurs, we might say, because a few owners with poor judgment put their money into factories that are too big for the town; that the collective budget of the consumers calls for just so much expenditure on the commodities of those owners and no more; that an error has been made in interpreting the public taste and anticipating demand, and that it will be punished. And it is not unlikely that other and sounder businesses will be affected and a regular depression precipitated on the town. According to that supposition it is simply the *unevenness* of capital expansion which cause[s] our present trouble, and which is the only kind of capital expansion we can possibly have. If the expansion were proportionate, it would not affect the relation between the items on the consumers' budget, but only give them a larger budget.

Even so, it would seem next to impossible to get this latter kind of expansion in an age when there are continually coming into the market new products which have to alter the consumers' budget if they are to be taken at all. There will be hardly the intelligence in human heads anywhere which can account closely for the effect of new products and anticipate the future distribution of the budget. If in Russia, where they would eliminate the scramble of competitive capital expansion and run the industries on collectivist principles, the governors propose to introduce a large range of articles for their consumers, Western style, they will probably have to ration the articles out, which is to budget the consumers very strictly, or else they too will be likely to have on their hands at any moment a number of overcapitalized industries, some of them abortive and some of them obsolescent.[4] Perhaps we shall see notices in this style: "Workers of Income Class ($-$) in District ($-$) will be expected within six months from date to

4. A handwritten correction complicates the meaning here. It appears that the original reads "their governors propose to introduce" and that Ransom crossed out the last two letters of "their," leaving "the governors propose to introduce" (as above). Perhaps the meaning would be made clearer by rendering the sentence thus: "If in Russia, where they would eliminate the scramble of competitive capital expansion and run the industries on collectivist principles, [and where] the governors propose to introduce a large range of articles for their consumers, Western style, they will probably have to ration the articles out . . ."

purchase one automobile each, Model (—). Deductions from pay will be made as follows."

We are in a bad way if overcapitalization consists only in a capital expansion which is uneven, and here-and-there excessive, for it cannot easily be avoided without bringing industrial progress to a dead stop in order to have it even. But we are really in a worse way, because overcapitalization goes much further than that. The theory of unevenness might be illustrated from the American depression of the '70s, when it was railroads and land companies that had overdeveloped, and when nevertheless their trouble seemed to communicate itself through all American business till it caused universal paralysis. But the theory quite breaks down before the present depression for the reason that *it is impossible to lay a finger on the guilty industries*. The overcapitalization is general; one industry is about as badly off as another. If even in 1928 there was an exceptional industry which was not overcapitalized, it would have done well to hide its light under a bushel, or it would be quickly invaded by new capital looking for investment in such volume as to overcapitalize it too. Such is the mobility of capital.

Overproduction, the consequence of overcapitalization, had become a commonplace of economic remark before the autumn of 1929; it was only its coming grand climactic effect that economists were too busy to notice. Some ready evidence for the layman on this point is contained in a volume of essays, *The Menace of Overproduction*.[5] It appeared in 1930 but its material was based on the statistics of the previous years. In this volume some captains of industry and some expert economists attached to industry wrote frankly and alarmingly about the excess of capital plant within their respective fields; they paid their respects, specifically, to such industries as those of bituminous coal, oil, and four textiles, farm products, radio equipment, steel; while still others with suitable qualifications discussed the general condition of overproduction. There was perfect agreement as to the peril; the productive plant was disproportionate not only to the existing market but to any

5. Scoville Hamlin, ed., *The Menace of Overproduction: Its Cause, Extent, and Cure* (New York: J. Wiley, 1930).

market which was likely to develop soon. As for definite proposals, several writers expressed the wish that the federal law might permit combinations "in restraint of trade," or at least in restraint of capital expansion. Some thought the need was for eliminating the marginal producer, but none indicated how this remedy was to be applied. Mr. Scoville Hamlin, the editor of the volume, concluded it with a résumé of the exhibit and a much more detailed proposal, principally to the effect that business should put less of its earnings into enlarging the plant and more into depreciation fund or reserves, which might serve to secure both the original capital investment and the employment of the personnel.

It is evidently the fact that all the businesses of the country may be overcapitalized and overproductive at the same time.

Mr. Henry Ford and Mr. Samuel Crowther, between them, have convictions about the way in which American business ought to be run, and their views, while very thoroughgoing, are scarcely distinguishable in essence from the new orthodoxy. Their books form an excellent set of scriptures for apologists of the new American idea. Mr. Hoover himself might have consulted them or their authors when, in his Inaugural Address, he expressed the opinion that we in America had developed an economic system whose "fundamental correctness" could not be doubted, and which was capable of abolishing poverty from this land.[6]

The Ford view is so far from being apprehensive of an overexpansion of business that it affirms that the expansion of business in America is not nearly fast and bold enough. Mass-production must be accelerated. When unsold products accumulate, the proper procedure is to produce in greater volume and lower the selling price. No effort must be spared to save labor cost[7] and in-

6. For President Hoover's address, see *Public Papers of the President: Herbert Hoover* (Washington, DC: United States Government Printing Office, 1974), 1:1–12. Samuel Crowther (1880–1947), American journalist, collaborated with Henry Ford.

7. Ransom did not pluralize "cost."

crease production by putting in new machines and processes; a whole plant must be scrapped when it begins to be obsolete. No attention must be paid to the competitors who will be driven out of business when a concern practices this policy; for only when individual enterprise is unrestrained will productivity have its maximum increase, and each concern may well attend to its own business in the assurance that there will be plenty of other business for the others to attend to. No business can undertake to guarantee its employees in their employment, but must hire and fire them in such numbers and such quality as the occasion requires, though a courageous business will probably never reduce their numbers permanently even if the improved equipment enables them to turn out many times as much production. The proper policy of a business towards its employees is to insist on highest and fastest performance but—and this is the only social doctrine in the whole profession of faith—to pay them high wages and give them maximum leisure in order that they may be good consumer-citizens for riding the forces of production.

This is the gospel of production as declared by a mechanical genius who likes the clatter and speed and the atmosphere of transition and insecurity that attend the operation of plants like that of the Ford Motor Company; who will scrap a plant worth many millions of dollars or dismiss 30,000 employees at a time without a qualm. The mortality both of capital investment and of employment will be heavy under these prescriptions. But capital investment represents the life effort of the investors, and employment is the bread of life to the laboring population, and it is a strenuous regime which calls for sacrificing them freely in the interests [of] some abstract perfection or even in the interest of future society. Such an economic system is too much like the internal combustion engine itself: its progress is by means of a series of explosions, which must be considered to be painful to the constituents of the engine if they have any sensibility. Besides, too much strain put upon the mechanism may kill the engine. The Ford plan would seem to invite this; and as a matter of fact the engine has stalled and will scarcely pick up again. Production was stepped up so rapidly, mass-production succeeded so well, that the productive plant got far ahead of the market and had to stop. Even that unit of it which is the Ford Motor Company had to stop.

———————

There is unquestionably a connection between overcapitalization and credit or monetary policy. The building of new capital plant does not have to wait upon the receipt of its cost in cash income from exiting plant, but may be financed partly on credit, and generally is. The credit issued by the bank is a risk taken on the chance that the business will earn a good return, and it is secured by the business' own paper. When good business men will risk their own cash in the venture, the bank is generally ready to risk its credit.

But if the business fails, the situation is doubly embarrassing. Not only does the owner lose his money, but the bank at once has to make good issue of credit. It must call in some of its other loans, and this causes a strain on the whole business community. This is the reason that bankruptcy is contagious, like smallpox; the weak businesses will collapse first under the pressure, and presently the sound ones will be attacked. It always proves on such occasions that there is a great deal of over-capitalization about in the special sense that there is a great deal of capital plant that had never been paid for. When so many businesses are vulnerable it is not possible for any considerable one of them to go down innocently.

The expansion of business takes place much more rapidly by reason of modern credit facilities than it otherwise would. The credit mechanism works in such a way as to contribute a wave-motion of expansion and contraction, or to intensify the up and down movements of the business cycle. When there is a fair balance between production and consumption, and business is earning well, credit is easy, and encourages a furious rate of expansion. Eventually, production is clearly in excess of demand, business houses begin to fail, there is no more credit to be had, and, on the contrary, everybody is called upon to pay his debts if he can. Most economists would assign a role to the state at this point. If a government is strong enough financially to swim against the stream, it may move to tighten up credit conditions when the expansion seems to be proceeding at a dangerous rate, and to make credit available when contraction has set in. It may check both the inflation of the up swing and the deflation of the down swing. In America the former policy was not followed during the great expansion period of the later '20s, because of the influence of the new economic theory of unbridled production; but the latter policy is being religiously followed during the present resulting depression. Neither policy, however, would hope to determine the whole general movement of business.

In England there is a school of economists, headed by Major Douglas,[8] who make much of a curious fact at this point. Credit is used solely to finance production, never to finance consumption. Consumption is quite private, its units are generally petty, it is destructive of the article consumed, and therefore the consumer can write no paper which banks will consider as security; while capital investment, on the other hand, results at once in physical plant whose evident intention is to bring in revenue and whose paper will pass at the bank. (British economists, in urging cancellation of the international debts owing to the United States, commonly repeat this consideration when they say that neither states nor banks can secure their loans unless these are for productive purposes.) No wonder production goes ahead of consumption when the financial system plays exclusively into its hands! But it does not yet appear that workable reforms can be proposed to meet this inequality. The financial system is an adjunct and tool of the productive system, and there is probably an end of the matter. The purpose of banks is to assist business, and the initiative of modern business has lain in the hands of the owners since the turn of the industrial revolution when business first became modern.

It may be thought that installment buying, which became popular as a desperate effort of producers to move their goods during the last decade, provides a credit to the consumers and is

8. Major Clifford Hugh Douglas (1879–1952), British engineer, helped develop the Social Credit economic reform proposal.

an exception to the rule above. The credit, however, is not issued by the banks or the state or any other third party but by the producers themselves. The extension of this credit only strains their own credit with the banks, for it is they and not the consumers whom the banks hold responsible.

––––––––––

A term which suggests itself here as convenient is: *Consumption lag*. Lags are in vogue with popular sciences just now; we are familiar with the wage lag, which defines the tendency of wages to rise more slowly than prices; and with the culture lag, which refers to the tendency of the culture-pattern to change more slowly than its economic framework. Consumption lag is one of the names for the great evil of our economy: a phenomenon in time: the tendency of consumption to increase more slowly than production.

Consumption lag and underconsumption refer to the same thing, but the former takes account of the all-important element of time. Admitted that the failure of C to balance P at the moment is temporary and not necessarily final, nevertheless in the period of waiting for C to approach equality with P there is a strain upon the P side to hold up, and the possibility that it will crash. Besides, the term consumption lag does not carry any reproach against the consumers, as underconsumption may seem to do. As a matter of fact, we did actually blame the wicked consumers for not consuming more of the good things provided by the admirable producers, in that maudlin campaign which was carried on in 1930 in order to bring about spending as usual. But we found before long that behind the refusal of the consumers to spend lay a real or economic disability.

But I prefer the term overcapitalization, if I have to name the evil in one word. The evil results from an act which takes place on the capital side of the fence; an act whose agents are the capitalizers or capitalists. The term is pointed. It may have a little of the Marxian tone, if we remember with what scorn the Marxians pronounce the terms capitalism, and capitalists; but I should not mind that association, for the Marxian analysis of the capitalistic economy is shrewd enough, though the remedy is too heroic for my taste. My term is a little more discriminating, however, for I do not pronounce such a broad term as a capitalism but only overcapitalization. I do not pronounce it with moral indignation at all. Overcapitalization is the evil of a system but it is inherent in the system, not in the personnel. When we consented to the system we consented to its implications.

———————

Modern business increasingly becomes big business. And big business has the advantage of superior economy of operation, and also the disadvantage of being the more liable to overcapitalization.

Big business begins with the discovery that a number of small capitals can operate more cheaply and effectively if combined in one large capital. Scientific organization or "management" has perhaps contributed as much as machine technology to the preëminence of the American productive society. The American F. W. Taylor devoted himself to the theory of scientific management, and the work is still being carried on by the Taylor Society of New York.[9] And many producers, such as Mr. Ford, have more or less independently worked out scientific management in practice.

Scientific management has reference to the scale of business organization. It works both vertically and horizontally. Vertically, when it organizes into one continuous unit all the processes by which an identical set of materials passes through many stages of preparation till it rests in the hands of the ultimate consumer. Horizontally, when it eliminates the local competition among businesses of the same kind by organizing what is relatively a monopoly. But whether you start with vertical or horizontal in-

---

9. Frederick Winslow Taylor (1856–1915), author of *Principles of Scientific Management*.

tentions, you generally finish with both. You build up such a fine capital with either kind of organization that you are able to take the next logical step and try the other kind. Perhaps the vertical organization is the more famous and ingenious of the two, and more particularly to the credit of American enterprise.

Of course scientific management does not stop there. Without any extensions of ownership it will undertake to run its business as economically as possible, eliminating surplus equipment and surplus labor wherever it can. This is just as real a work of economy though it is not so spectacular.

Big business on this plan is effective in delivering its goods more cheaply, and therefore it gets the trade. It presents society with an absolute reduction in price, and at the same time it presents the owners with a savings in cost. But at whose expense does it realize this saving?

From the standpoint of its vertical action, it eliminates the profits, salaries, and wages of middlemen; and from the standpoint of its horizontal action it eliminates the profits, salaries, and wages of excessive personnel here and there. Its effect therefore is precisely like that of the labor-saving machine: it cancels some of the income that was dribbling into the hands of small owners and executives and laborers. It evicts them for the moment from the industrial order.

But it has to pay for it. The saving in question goes to the owners, who are big owners, and in their hands becomes mostly free capital asking to be invested; it used to go to little owners or employees, in whose hands it was spending money.

––––––––

The chain stores are a good example of a scientific management that reduces cost without the benefit of any new machinery in particular. They are big business applied to merchandising. They represent mainly, perhaps, a horizontal organization that substitutes combination under one ownership for a group of competitors on the same market. But they tend more and more to the vertical:

that is, to going back and taking part in the actual production and preparation of the goods. Either way they affect considerable economies in final cost. They can actually sell cheaper, and naturally they get the trade.

They squeeze out that small "independent" who have not their advantages. Many sentimental objections are being offered on behalf of the local merchants of the home town, but there is also a very strong economic objection that I have scarcely seen advanced. The profits of merchandising are not now distributed among a great number of little men, where, according to representations that seem likely enough, they would mostly be spent harmlessly enough on comforts, or given away to the local charities, or paid in better wages to the merchants' help—but not devoted religiously to savings and investment. They are now distributed among a smaller number of wealthy men, where for the most part they will automatically be marked for re-investment. Insofar as a chain of stores proves to be a good investment for capital, it will attract first its own income, then that of other capital. The original chain is likely to overbuild and hurt its own earnings, but even if it does not the same results will be accomplished when envious competitors enter the field with chains of their own. Chain stores are a fairly new thing, but not so new as to have escaped the general overcapitalization. Periodically the chain stores, like other businesses, will all hit the rocks together.

The chain stores system, then, looks good in that it replaces what might be called an absolute overcapitalization of merchandising, since it can get the same work done at a smaller actual expenditure. But it replaces a capitalization which was fairly stable with one which is progressive and therefore highly unstable and dangerous. When the business of the town was conducted by small independent merchants, any business failure that occurred would be occasional, local, unrelated, and could be absorbed by the business community. The failures of great chains, on the other hand, will not be local, they will be national, and they will all come at once in that moment when business has come full circle; they will add to a general distress.

In spite of the interrelation of the businesses, and strangely co-existing with it, is the fact that they are in competition. Each industry would improve its quota in the general consumers' budget, and then each unit of the industry would improve its share of that quota.

The investor may be fully aware of the perils of competition, and behind the competition of a general overcapitalization already in existence. He studies the more doubtfully the problem of his investment, but he makes it all the same. He cannot help it.

It is impossible to tell exactly at what point a fresh investment in a given business will constitute an excessive investment and start that business downhill on the road to overproduction and failure of earnings. The expectation as to earning-power with which a unit of capital is credited in the business is based on last month's dividend, or last year's earnings, or a ten-year record, but that is a precarious basis to depend on; especially if the capital plant is being greatly enlarged, with this capitalist and that capitalist putting in his new money. If only capital investments were built out of some simple homogeneous physical stuff as a lake is built out of gallons of water, and their earning power could be estimated in advance with as much confidence as the power to be generated at the dam, then it might be possible for the first excessive dollar to be detected, and no second dollar to follow vainly after it. But investments are not like that. The field is too vast and irregular to be charted, the forces are incalculable, and there is a fatal lapse of time before the effects can show themselves decisively. The investor, even if he has the assistance of the leading brokers and bankers of his section, must go it blind.

But here is the point. He knows that some private business will continue to earn even after there is overcapitalization and depression in business as a whole. Even today there are corporations paying dividends comparable with those of 1928. Competition means that each business has a chance though there is not room for all. There may be times when nearly all of them are earning well, but in other times the competition is one of life and death. Some will die but others will survive, and a few will flourish without interruption. Which will be the lucky ones? The capitalists who make the final disposition of investment monies cannot but be fascinated by that question, even if they are aware that the field which they are contemplating is overcrowded. They study long and hard for the traits which permit a business to live through the storm. Each one is determined to put his money on a business of that sort; to manage well, to be more efficient than his competitors, and to win at their expense. Though the capitalists might remind themselves in so many words incessantly—and they know it intuitively very well—that the death of capital is due to overcapitalization, they could never be sure which capital was doomed, and they would continue to embark upon the competition that was going to prove mortal for somebody's capital in the hope that it would not be mortal for theirs.

Such a situation gives little scope for mathematical or mechanical calculations. If we require a figure of speech, we may liken the competition to the wars of men. Suppose for a moment, as the Malthusians have supposed, and as the event must now and then have been, that in a given area the population has increased faster than its means of subsistence. There are too many people and they will have to fight it out for their food. They may fight as individuals in a free-for-all, or they may fight as racial and national groups. But there is no alternative. They must fight. Each man or each group fights in the hope of winning, and it cannot be demonstrated in advance that he will lose. The weak man or the weak group will probably make alliances to improve position: the number of hungry mouths is not thereby reduced. The issue is always uncertain. But if we are meditating the issue well before the fighting has begun, it is much more uncertain. You cannot tell when, nor where, nor on what provocation it will begin, nor how the fighters will align themselves, nor whether they will fight a long slow war of attrition or decide it in one brief but bloody campaign. When it is over, the historians are apt to remark sagely, "The efficient ones destroyed the inefficient ones." But this is to say nothing, this is only a circumlocution. If they could have told us before the event who were the efficient ones, they would have said something. But they never can. Perhaps that is why wars are still fought. At any rate that is why economic competition, with all its mortality, still defines the relation of one capital to another.

Chapter 3

SOME PROPOSED EXTINGUISHERS

Nobody at this moment will deny that our capitalistic economy suffers from an organic defect, somewhere or other. Some economists will be inclined to think it is incurable, as it causes these periodic breakdowns of business, and as this the latest one seems to be worse than those that preceded it. Others, sanguine of temperament perhaps, assume that it can be remedied, and propose the remedies. Even the most pessimistic critic is honor-bound to examine these proposals if he is not to be a complete misanthrope.

The nature of the remedy depends naturally upon the analysis of the trouble. In the previous chapter I have urged that depressions, marked by general failure of earnings and a high figure of unemployment, result from a tendency to overcapitalization, or excessive capital spread, which is inherent in capitalistic economy. From this point of view let us look at some of the more famous proposals we have heard for amending capitalism. To what extent will they act as extinguishers of capital excess, bring the capital equipment back to normal, and keep it there?

There may be a sense, of course, in which it is not necessary to tinker with capitalism at all. Capitalism has been reckoned to be a sturdy economy, capable of keeping going whatever we may do, though its violent ups and downs may be uncomfortable for us who live under it. It might be described as a natural economy rather than an artificial one, since the traditional policy which statesmen have religiously followed has consisted in leaving it alone, or even in defending it from being interfered with. This natural system, then, is busy throwing off its own trouble, and will probably succeed, though this is evidently about the hardest recovery it has been called upon to make. The marginal capital is actually being abandoned; it is going into voluntary and involuntary liquidation, it is being sold up to satisfy the creditors, it is being scrapped. This is nature's way of repairing her own economy. An excess of capital is like an excess of population: it dies off. So capitalism will recover unaided. And that, to some people, is all there is to it.

But others figure that the disease of capitalism is progressive, and will destroy it if nothing is done by the doctor; and at any rate that we, who are reputed to occupy a position both within nature's scheme and above it, might try to improve upon that scheme and make it produce for us a better welfare. We do not like the experience of being caught up within these great natural convulsions at the expense of our dignity, our comfort, and our lives.

––––––––––

(1) The pleasantest of all possible cures for a state of things which is defined by idle capital and unemployed labor is: *New industries*. But to prescribe them is one thing and to fill the prescription is another. "All that this patient needs is a new field in which he may be absolutely free to express his remarkable energies": but where is the field? New industries, if they could start up on a large scale and run successfully, might rather quickly absorb the idle capital and labor, and most of us would be happy again. But new industries do not come because they are called. They may hang back. They are incalculable.

It is just for this reason that capitalism cannot really be considered to have a sound constitution; it has a taint in its blood; it is liable, and will be liable all its life, to the malady of overcapitalization. For capitalism always liberates new capital for investment; and investors look always for new industries but, when they do not find them, fall back upon the existing industries; which is overcapitalization. Even if the look for new industries is successful in short order, and the free capital fixes itself at once in the new form without doing any damage to the old industries, the taint is still there. For what purpose is the new capital entering the new industry? To reproduce itself, of course. It is to yield to the owners an income in excess of their spending needs; and that is the birth of another free capital, and the beginning of another cycle of the same order. Old industries call for new industries, which become old industries and call for new industries, which again call for new industries, *ad infinitum*; a grand example of the infinite series. The philosophy of capitalism is evidently a blind faith in what it calls progress. It is always depending on new industries to turn up and always, when they do not turn up, running its head into the trap of overcapitalization. Nothing can save capitalism from its own hurt except some providential dispensation to the effect that there shall always be handsome new industries waiting to support the free capitals which the old capitals, with their appalling fertility, are determined to beget. But capitalism trusts providence too far if it expects this. Its history, which is filled with crises and crashes, shows the vanity of the expectation. Its future is likely to be not less tragic but more tragic than its past.

That there will presently be some new industries, we may suppose. Something better than miniature golf links, which did not provide much salvation in the summer of 1930; better than the short-lived and far too inexpensive pastime of Yo-yo; better even than free-wheeling and such developments in automobile equipment. There is hope in the manufactures made possible by the new physics of electrons and the vacuum tube. Much of the existing fixed capital is clearly marked for destruction, but at any rate there will be some new fixations for the free capitals to come which will make the wheels of production go round. Only, we may with the greatest confidence make the reservation: the crisis will come again.

It is in the new industries that we have the purest examples of the law that $P = C$. They come into existence in a world where the balance between P and C is precarious, with plant expanding faster than market and threatening to become overproductive and unprofitable. Or they come into a world, like the present world, where overproduction and stagnation have already set in, where the new free capital (which is being excreted by the old industries at a lessening rate) does not know where to fix itself, where the unemployed (who are being expelled at an increasing rate) cannot find occupation. The new venture steps into this breach. It absorbs the available capital and the available credit, it recruits from the unemployed. The danger of overcapitalization is shelved for the time being, with capital earnings from the old industries tending to invest in the new industry, along with, of course, a handsome set of earnings from the new industry itself. I repeat: for the time being.

And now Mr. Ford announces that he will devote all his resources to putting out a new car which will employ many thousands of idle laborers, bring about a business turnover of perhaps billions of dollars, and help to revive American industry. If he can carry out this project, economists will call him blessed. Our only misgivings will arise when we wonder how long it will be this time before Mr. Ford, in the downrightness of his capitalistic methods, will have saturated the market which he proposes to create, and will have to slow down his plant and begin to discharge his workmen again.

The economics of the Ford project are complicated by the question of whether it might not be classified as only an expansion within an old industry. After all, Mr. Ford's regular business is the manufacturer [*sic*] of cars, which are not now a novelty. But then he has been making few cars recently, his old labor colony has mostly joined the army of the unemployed, and his new car will be new at least in the sense that it will need what is very largely a new plant for its production. As between an old industry and a new industry, this one will be perhaps about half and half. But the term new industry must generally be used rather broadly. The new Ford car will be competing necessarily with old cars already on the market, and it will be displacing old Ford cars. But an industry that is new at every point must compete with old industries in the sense that it wants the biggest share possible of the consumers' budget. It competes more pointedly with the industries whose products are in the same general field with its own. Cars compete with all previous locomotive devices, but also with radio sets and musical instruments and theatricals as the means of pastime. The merit of a good new industry is that its product, in the salesman's sense, will go, it will break up the stagnation of business, it will trouble the waters. It may have a beneficent effect even on the industries with which it is most closely in competition, by the mere fact that it revives the habit of trade, and if it should drive them presently out of business, it will be furnishing them with the easiest death they can die; for with the business revival made possible by the new industry there is a profitable direction to be taken by such capital as can be rescued from the defunct industries, and by the workmen who must go out of them. The new industry that can produce a fine commodity and flourish is welcomed by the business world no matter how many unflourishing industries it will displace, for the unflourishing industries are not of much use to the business world anyway.

The hour waits for the new industries. Let them come, let them establish themselves as firmly as possible. The relief they bring will be belated, and it will be temporary, but it will be kindly received.

––––––

(2) A supposed cure for a local overcapitalization, which in this age is the overcapitalization of our American industries, is: *Expansion of the foreign trade*. Such an idea at least is in the heads of many rather unobservant people; though it is being rapidly knocked out of the heads of realistic economists who see in what state the international markets are today. The disposal of a great deal of our surplus production on the foreign markets may be something to

long for, but scarcely anything to hope for, and hardly worth trying for very hard. The reason is a simple one: the foreign nations are themselves overcapitalized and overproductive. The universal vogue of tariff walls shows that.

Nations, if we may personify them, are as naïve as individuals in their practice of capitalism. The intention of a self-conscious nation to have a favorable balance of trade is like the intention of a private capitalist to clear some free capital out of his business for fresh disposal. This fact is represented in the economic maxim which says that a nation which sells more goods than it buys receives for the excess its equivalent in gold; the gold which the nation earns is a net profit corresponding to the clearings of the private business. But it is not an unmixed blessing. In withholding part of the total income of your private business for investment you are delaying the purchase fund from taking up your products; and in taking the gold out of the country to which you have [sold, you are impoverishing] your buyer and making him less able to buy in the future.[1] We have all been instructed in how the gold will make for cheap money and higher prices in the country which gets it, and dear money and low prices in the country which loses it, until the buyer nation can no longer afford to buy but is rather in a position to sell, and the flow of trade begins to reverse itself; just as the free capital earned by an owner will go back into plant and waste itself in overcapitalization. Both processes undo themselves.

There is an exception to the law that an unbalanced trade means the export of gold from the debtor country, but it does not mean that the balance can continue permanently in favor of the other country. If the nation which buys cannot go on indefinitely paying in gold, the other nation may leave the gold in the form of permanent investments for which it holds the bonds. It will then own so many liens on the internal wealth of the debtor nation and in effect it will be waiving the principal of the debt in the hope of receiving faithfully the interest. This is what Britain did with many

1. The part in brackets is a reasonable conjecture of what has been partially cut off in the original manuscript.

countries for over half a century, as an offset to foreign sales which were greatly in excess of its purchases. But what is the nature of these investments? They are capital plants erected for production, and it may be supposed that they will often be plants more or less duplicating the kind of plants which the creditor nation had at home, and indeed under the supervision of the creditor nation, on the understanding that the same investments which have prospered in one country will prosper in another. But the time inevitably comes when these new plants will be actually competing with the old ones. The local industries founded on foreign money are technical lessons in industry, the beginnings of a national industrial establishment. The debtor people has been very kindly furnished with instruction in the capitalistic economy. Neither Britain nor any other country can pour its restless productive capital into a backward country without building up there a capital establishment along the usual lines. The financing of railroads, or the opening of mines and banks for the debtors, is not an innocent investment without consequences; for railroads are the beginnings of industry, calling for business to come and camp along the track, while minerals call for metallurgical plants, and banks intend to promote industry of every kind. So the country which has been helped along in this way is likely at last to be tolerably self-sufficient. It begins to dispense with the goods from the creditor country which it now can furnish for itself, then it finds itself able to enter the neutral markets and cut into its own guardian's trade, and finally it has the assurance to invade the great stronghold itself from whence all its industrial development sprang.[2] Britain has seen this very thing happen. The British, as the manufacturers of the world, were forced to become its brokers and bankers in order to take care of their credits; but as bankers and brokers they were inevitably developers and teachers of capitalism, and now— here they are! Their own national plant cannot dispose of its

2. The original reads, "It begins to dispense with the goods from the creditor which it can now furnish for itself . . ." Above "creditor" is superscripted "country" with no mark indicating where precisely Ransom wished the word to be placed.

production in the face of competition from the national plants that they have helped to bring into the world. This is the way in which capitalism applied on the national scale is bound to overreach itself and come to grief.

———

There is one way perhaps by which the nations could expand their foreign trade without fear of competition and hard feeling: if each nation were accorded a perfect monopoly on its particular industries and there were no overlapping. The United States, for example, might make all the shoes, while Britain made all the clothes; each of us could make all we liked of our article without hurting the other. If the industrially minded nations had come together fifty years ago and solemnly agreed upon some allotment of industries, and if the agreement could have been maintained, then there would today be a foreign market guaranteed for every nation and not requiring to be won and held under the most desperate competition. But there would be some trifling difficulties. For instance, we might be supplying the world with all the shoes it could wear and still not be fully occupied; we would still have the problem of what to do with the money we had made and the labor that our efficient technique had emancipated; we might be just as discontented as we are at this moment; and we would probably raise the question whether the agreements of one generation ought to be allowed to hold the succeeding generations in fetters.

But there have been no such monopolies accorded. It is contrary to the genius of capitalism, which is individualistic, aggressive, competitive, versatile, and expansive. The only safe monopolies that nations have are natural ones: industries that require mineral resources, or soil and climate of a certain sort. And when free capital is specially abundant and has nothing better to do, it will move heaven and earth to see if it cannot produce elsewhere the goods on which some nation seemed to possess a natural monopoly. It is announced that an American company has learned how to make synthetic rubber in commercial quantities, and has only to bring the cost of production down somewhat to make it profitable, and to displace the rubber which now has to be imported. The bulk of the trade among the great nations is in the products of competitive industry, not monopoly.

Sometimes we hear it said that we have a vast potential market in China, when that country recovers from its revolutions. But China cannot buy heavily of our wares without developing some wares to offer in exchange, or permitting us to help her develop some wares for exchange. We are told that the Chinese make excellent factory hands, having plenty of intelligence and tireless strength, and being contented with low wages; that China is going to be a great manufacturer of textiles, for example. In that case China will have the wherewithal to buy from us; but only if we are willing to take the Chinese textiles in exchange. There might be such a campaign against this betrayal of our own textile manufacturers, to say nothing of legislation in the shape of a tariff, that the trade with China would not materialize. The industries which sold to China—the farms, for instance—would be helped by it no more than the textile industries would be hurt. Of course the Chinese are a peculiar people, and on their textile products might conceivably put some Chinese characteristic which would appeal to our consumers, and which could not easily be duplicated by our textile plants. But they would be replacing our own products somewhere or other; Chinese clothing and American clothing could hardly be worn at the same time; and even if they could, the money spent on the Chinese half of the wardrobe might have been spent on something manufactured at home. However that may be, the international trade tends less and less to be trade in national specialties, and more and more in standard or staple articles that are produced just as well in one country as another. The national plants duplicate each other shamelessly.

Therefore the economists who are not on behalf of restoring free trade among the industrial nations at this time of day are guilty of an anachronism in their thinking. If our industries are ailing because they are overproductive, we must stop to remember that this is the condition of the industries of other nations. All the great nations want to sell and not to buy, which is scarcely the background for a flourishing international trade. It is as if our own nationals, starting abroad with goods to sell, encountered somewhere about half way the nationals of other countries bearing the same types of goods to sell to us; both nationals might as well turn round and go home.

———————

(3) The capitalists, the movers of the whole economy called capitalism, may be relied upon to do what they can to find new industries into which their free capital may flow harmlessly; they will also divert into the foreign trade as much of it as the trade will stand, and probably more; and yet they know that something else is required to cure the condition of overcapitalization. At this point, when now they have been forced to confess that the trouble is more serious than they had supposed, they talk of a remedy which is radical indeed. They talk of nothing less than holding back their investments and adapting the producing capital to the actual market. In short, they talk of capitalizing their industries on a rational basis.

The third remedy for overcapitalization therefore is a policy called: *Rationalization*. If this is a stiff and ugly word, there is another which comes to much the same thing: *Planning*.

It seems a pity for good capitalists to talk about thus reforming themselves, as if capitalism might become a self-damping system, unless they are in deadly earnest, and have seen a great light. And that is not sufficiently probable. It cannot be unless they are willing to cease to be capitalists themselves and able to commit the other capitalists now and forever to the great renunciation—the renunciation of the right to take compound interest and to invest profits. In calling themselves rationalists they must be aware, even if they are big business men and high Republican officials, that capitalism is not rational as it stands. But they probably do not realize, or at least do not admit, just how far short of rational it is, nor what a revolution would be required to make it so.

As a matter of fact, it is significant that the downright and serious talk about planning and rationalization rarely comes from the capitalists themselves. It comes from disinterested political economists; or it comes from anti-capitalists, those who have been disposed by the march of capitalism, such as labor unionists. Planning, which varies in the degree of the severity of its measures, involves at least the surrender of some freedom on the part of the capitalist, the abandonment of some of his contractual rights; and planning is something recommended by the non-capitalists! Their proposals are generally excellent from their own point of view, but how will they appear to the private owner of a marginal business, or the executives of any business who have been instructed to earn dividends?

In these early stages planning exhibits a great variety of schemes. It may propose, with the labor unions, that owners pay higher wages and reduce the hours of labor; that they insure their employees against unemployment; that they build pretty cottages and plant lawns for their employees; that they play baseball with their employees. But sooner or later planning comes to the most important reform on its schedule, the fundamental reform of capitalism as I have analyzed it. What about the excessive capital plants that owners continually bring into existence? Planning would not be a serious undertaking at all if it did not propose to hold down capital expansion. This will be real rationalization.

Rationalization in this sense is to be undertaken first by the whole of a given industry, where it is to consist in obtaining an agreement of the competing capitalists already on the ground, and an allocation of the market among them which is to give them virtual monopolies. This is a sort of extension to the industry of that scientific management by which little businesses combine into big business. But we must remember that a big business is still a private capital girding itself up for competition with other capitals. Does rationalization then mean, as is claimed for it sometimes, that capitalists with private motives are to be converted into co-operationists with social motives? This would be a fabulous change, and the birth of an entirely new psychology. But it hardly means that. The motive of the capitalists in an industry submitting to rationalism—if there were one—still looks quite private; they seem to be signing a truce to cease competition, in the moment of business depression, in order to save their capitalists. But when they begin to make profits again, what will they do with them? Under the agreement they can increase their respective capitalizations only according to a schedule, or they cannot increase them at all. In either case there will be excess income for investment; and if the agreement keeps it from going back into its parent capital, it must go elsewhere, and help to wreck some other industry.

At this point we hear that rationalization is to apply not only to the single industry, but to all the industries of the nation at once; and is not this a piece of truly political economy, does it not amount to the handsomest abdication on the part of the capitalists? It would indeed be a remarkable phenomenon: capitalists receiving excess income and yet not feeling free to put it anywhere. Or would there be a place to put it? The only thing they could do with it would be to pour it into investments producing for the foreign markets. But while the home investments might now be enjoying some stability, the new foreign ones would be growing excessive. And since a home market is a foreign market for all the countries but one, and all the countries might be rationalizing at once, we would soon have a worldwide overcapitalization, which in no sense is nicer than a national overcapitalization, but less nice.

And if the rationalists tell us they will extend their principle to the international trade, and stop up the last outlet for free capital investment, then indeed they are talking about Utopia; but a socialistic or communistic one; a system in which the capitalists could not dispose of their own profits and which is, virtually, not a capitalistic system.

It is pleasant to think of the capitalists lying down like little lambs together, but it is not a picture to be taken seriously at first sight. Capitalists may be in the mood at a certain stage of the business cycle, but wait five years! Capitalists in distress are weary of the battle, they want to herd together, and their blood runs cold;

but a little prosperity will act as a wonderful invigorator. The father of rationalization is said to have been Walter Rathenau.[3] But he was director in 85 German concerns and 21 foreign ones, an extraordinary position which was bound to prejudice his view of competition.

———————

One of the most realistic planners in this country is Mr. George Soule, who does not expect planning to make its way very rapidly, nor ask it to do too much at once.[4] He contemplates a purely voluntary system of planning and he knows that he must convert to it the owners themselves, who are the only powers worth mentioning in our industrial society. He therefore discusses at length the motive behind business, and he would like to discover that planning is not really inconsistent with the complex of motives usually entertained. The "economic man" was supposed to be a creature motivated solely by the desire for profit, and under this simple definition he was an abstraction and a myth; planning does not have to reckon with such a man. The substitute which Mr. Soule offers for his concept is the "organizing man." The captain of industry does not care necessarily about having a big income for his personal use, he cares about organizing a great business and conducting it efficiently. But surely Mr. Soule must notice that this term is not passive but active; the captain of industry proposes to do his own organizing. The "organizing disposition of mankind" upon which Mr. Soule would impose his program of planning is not the same thing as a disposition for being organized. The two dispositions are in fact antithetical: one is individual and one is social.

Capitalism as we know it is an economic system only by the grace of God; under it owners with perfectly private motives have

———

3. Walther (not Walter) Rathenau (1867–1922), German industrialist and foreign minister during the Weimar Republic.

4. George Soule, liberal journalist during the New Deal era and author of *A Planned Society* (New York: Macmillan, 1932).

managed by some blessed providence to compete and yet to co-exist and even to re-inforce each other—up to a certain point. What they must surrender now, however, if industrial society is to be saved, is precisely their individualism, the free spread of the age over that part of the business world which each one would like to organize. They may surrender it voluntarily, but it is not likely, for it is foreign to their business psychology.

Mr. Soule makes much use of the successful piece of planning accomplished during the war by the War Industries Board without grieving the spirits of our capitalists overmuch. But there is a difference between war planning and peace planning which he scarcely mentions. The Board's primary object was to meet the unparalleled consumption-needs of the United States and her allies; it therefore demanded production, more production, production which could not be speeded up sufficiently. Nothing could have been more congenial to the capitalistic temperament. The Board was offering capitalists a positive policy of expression, not a negative policy of repression; it was asking them to increase production, not hold back.

Mr. Soule does not like to talk about restricting production at all, but hopes that will be unnecessary if planning can secure its proper distribution. Nevertheless he is obliged to deprecate the practice of increasing private plant whenever market conditions make it certain that his increase can only pay for itself by destroying some competitive plant. That is exactly what has been taking place. The owners undertook too much of a spread, they did too much organizing, they overbuilt their businesses. Each one enjoyed his own spread and hoped he could maintain it even if it interfered with the competitors' spread. Therefore, Mr. Soule will be obliged to stop them from the practice by his technique of dissuasion. (Planners are like old-fashioned temperance workers in that work must be more dissuasive than persuasive; and they may in discouragement wind up in the same way, as prohibitionists.) Now we have been given to understand that the great step which one of the European cartels or consortia takes, and which it is formed (by a mixture of suasion and coercion) expressly for the sake of taking, is the drastic limitation of the capital plant of its industry. Its owners need not grow ambitious, for they are held down to their quotas of the total volume of business; and though it is promised that they may expand later on, it will only be when the market calls for more of their products, and the expansion will not be so much a free scramble to see which one can get there first as a proportionate expansion for all. On the part of the owners this is being obedient or even loyal to an organization; it is by no means the full-blooded act of organizing which American business men relish. If Mr. Soule or the Taylorian engineers of any other disinterested political economists can win their consent to such a scheme, it will be splendid. But it will have to go against the grain. Our business men are not ants, they are not even Prussians or Fascistic or Russians, they are American individualists. It is so hard to imagine that the sugar of phrases like "organizing man" will stop them from detecting that the pill is made out of plain socialism.

———————

(4) It is unlikely that capitalism will save itself from overcapitalization by taking thought; that is, by trying harder to find new industries capable of absorbing the new capital; or by unloading it upon industries producing for the foreign market; or by withholding it from investment under a schedule of rational capitalization. Capitalism is hardly calculated to cure its own ills. Let us see what sort of prescription may be administered from the outside.

The first of these prescriptions will be clearly: *Labor unionism*. It is not only a measure applied from the outside, it represents opposition, force, class warfare—the non-capitalists fighting to impose a rule of conduct upon the capitalists. It is true they are not theorizing about the necessity of preventing a great fraction of the total income fund from recapitalizing in the hands of the owners. But when they reach into this fund and extract additional amounts of it for themselves, they are preventing most effectively. Labor, fighting for higher wages, compels capitalism to submit to a sort of rationalization, and to maintain a better ratio between consumption power and production.

It may not suit us temperamentally to take such a position, but as political economists we cannot do otherwise than favor a bigger and better unionism. Personally, it may be that I loathe, on behalf of the workers, both the necessity and the technique of unionism. But this is the one effective instrument which we have seen consecrated to the cause of improving the workers' share in the income.

The unions must make their own fight, the state cannot do much for them without betraying capitalism and playing favorites. The political economist may give them their blessing, and create for them a sympathetic public opinion, but they can scarcely proceed to the legislation of wages and still respect the institution of private property. What the state can do is to be careful that its police and courts are available to protect from violence, with perfect impartiality, the persons and properties of the owners and the persons and properties of the strikers. This rule will work both ways. The war of the classes here is to be fought strictly within the economic field.

It remains to be seen how far labor can go in increasing its share of income through economic action strictly. Probably not so far as unionists once supposed. Labor unionism since the war, and during a period of rapid improvement in technology, when labor has been thrown upon the market, has lost ground; it has less bargaining power. Many of its friends are so sensitive to this that they would advocate for unionism, not economic action merely, but political action. But that is another story; we shall come to that presently. The least that labor can do in the meantime is to organize for economic action.

Labor may as well remember in any case that its own income in the form of wages can never quite determine the distribution nor the disposition of the owners' income in the form of return on capital. The critical feature of owners' incomes is their inequality. The owners' blocs of stock are unequal, and so are their incomes. But to him that hath shall be given. It is not a mere inequality but a progressive one. Of two unequal incomes a larger fraction of the larger one will be available for re-investment, and so the larger stock will gain on the smaller, and the large income will do the same. Therefore a drain on owners' income in the form of wages can never prevent some owners from making excessive capital investments, and no wage formula which the unions may impose will ever take up the exact excess of income that is capitalized when it ought not to be capitalized. The danger of unionism will have some effect on the movement of the business cycle but not stop it.

———————

(5) Another remedy applied from the outside to check overcapitalization is: *Humanitarian levies upon capitalistic income*. This may be an unusual classification of several very ordinary measures, and require some explanation.

Society has advanced in the quickness of its conscience, which now requires that it relieve its poor and distressed. Where is the money to come from? It must come from those who have it for the benefit of those who do not have it; or it must come from those who have much for the benefit of those who have little. It is a levy upon income, but if it falls peculiarly or with a graduated force upon owners' income, we are justified in referring to a humanitarian levy on that income.

There are many citizens who are willing to levy upon the rich for the benefit of the poor. They are perhaps not the orthodox political economists. As such, these we must distinguish sharply from humanitarians; they are interested in the "wealth of nations" rather than in the comparative wealth of any classes within the nation;[5] they want to see a great aggregate wealth, and a secure wealth

5. Ransom's corrections are unclear. The original reads thus: "They are perhaps not the orthodox political economists, as such these we must distinguish sharply from humanitarians, they are interested in the 'wealth of nations' rather than in the comparative wealth of any classes within the nation." The passage may also be rendered thus: "They are perhaps not the orthodox political economists, as such. These we must distinguish sharply from humanitarians; they are interested in the 'wealth of nations' rather than in the comparative wealth of any classes within the nation."

whose income flows regularly, and such things as that; they do not favor in advance either of the parties in the war of the classes.

And it could hardly be said that modern society as a whole, when it makes a humanitarian levy upon the capitalistic income, is trying to overthrow capitalism or even cause it to stumble. A humanitarian levy for the poor is not going to accomplish much for them; it is not a reform of society which is going to put the high persons on the bottom and the low persons on the top, or to put them on the same level, or to make any relative stratification of them whatever. It leaves things where they were so far as interference with the natural economy is concerned. It simply discharges a humanitarian obligation, as painlessly as possible. It removes or improves an ugly blot upon the working of the capitalistic system but does not want to destroy that system.

It affects the evil of overcapitalization only to the extent that it drains the income of the capitalists and diverts so much of it from its normal destiny of investment. In ordinary times this drain is not heavy. The impulse behind it is merely, once more, humanitarian. The desire to prevent overcapitalization is a more subtle thought which is hardly in the public consciousness at all, though that is the consideration that brings it to our attention at this moment.

I shall mention two particular levies. The first is for the purpose of insurance of wages. The other consists in taxation for any purpose whatever, so far as it bears particularly upon capitalistic income.

———————

Insurance against unemployment, like most other forms of insurance, is generally accepted as a desirable thing, for individuals exposed as they are in this world to risks, especially to workmen exposed as they are to waves of unemployment resulting from the excessive ambition of capitalists. But it must be remembered that not even insurance is safe. The insurance of employment is so exposed to such contingencies that it is scarcely subject to scientific calculation by the actuaries. Under any insurance scheme the insured puts in—or has somebody put in for him—small amounts at regular intervals and gets out, when his time of need officially arises, a fixed amount which is not necessarily the amount he paid in. The insurance fund makes no addition to the joint wealth, for though it may make an addition to the wealth of an individual, this is at the expense of the wealth of the others; there must be losers in this scheme if there are to be any winners. And insurance never prevents the occurrence of the thing insured against, whether it be death, or fire, or unemployment. If the thing occurs to all of them at the same time, they or their heirs will not receive what they have been led to expect; they will get out at most what they have put in; the fund will probably be dissipated at once and the insurance project will come to an end. Insurance works where the thing insured against occurs with a fairly small but consistent frequency.

We have not made up our minds yet about unemployment insurance in this country. But suppose we do come to it; what form of insurance which serves the purpose of relieving the unemployed will also look the best to a political economist, as a measure which will tend to check this unemployment? Whether capitalists say "overcapitalization" when they are asked about the cause of unemployment, or say something else, it is necessarily something that the capitalists, who are in sole charge of the system, do with their management; economists therefore are apt to consent that the payment of the premiums on the insurance of employees might do well to fall in part on the capitalistic income. That is the kind of unemployment insurance that is being urged upon us. It is bound to have an effect upon overcapitalization, precisely like the increase of wages which has been won by some strong union at the expense of the normal capitalistic income.

But the insurance levy, like the wage scale, can hardly be so elastic and so pointed as to wipe out precisely the danger income in all the industries, big and little, strong, and weak, and for all the private owners.

A point of administration. If the economic value of the insurance levy lies in its tendency to prevent overcapitalization, it will be inconsistent with its purpose if the insurance fund is expected to appreciate through investment. It should not be like ordinary insurance funds in this respect. Our life insurance companies bear an important part of the responsibility for our disastrous cycle because they invest their money. An ordinary life insurance policy today is not merely an insurance policy but a certificate of investment, paying dividends. This may be good private business for the insured person. But as political economists we would like to check investments. Insurance against unemployment is the taking of a chance precisely against the depression phase of the business movement. But this phase is the consequence of overinvestment, and nothing is accomplished by the insurance scheme if the money which might have been invested by the capitalists in the first place is taken away from them only to be invested by somebody else.

———————

The other levy upon capitalistic income of which I will speak is taxation, for whatever purpose its revenue may be used. To affect a reduced rate of capital investment, the tax must fall principally or altogether upon the guilty incomes, which are the large ones, or the capitalistic ones; and that is exactly the practice to which we have come for one of our principal forms of taxation: the graduated income tax. I supposed, again, that we really adopted it out of pure humanitarianism. "The rich can pay this tax more easily than the poor." As orthodox political economists we would doubtless have to ask the state to take its revenues from all income at the same rate. But we may well be glad if there has been established in defiance of our strict political economy a different principle at the expense of owners' income which has not destroyed business, nor come near destroying it, and yet must have had some effect in damping its vicious tendencies.

The reason that taxation will scarcely destroy capitalism is that a state does not require enough money for its normal functions to drain off the excess income. If it did, we might as well let the state run our business for us and be done, for there would be no profit in it. In bad times the weight of a tax is heavy on the capitalists, but in those times it is heavy on everybody. (Evidently taxation is regularly too easy on the big owners during prosperity, and too hard on them during depressions.)

The greater the income, the greater the fraction of it taken: that is our modern idea of taxation. It looks as if it had been proposed by somebody bent on hitting the very incomes that did the damage. So far as a tax may seize and sequester the dangerous money, this looks like the perfect one. But it is not quite perfect, I think. It is really a lucky makeshift. Why should not the tax undertake to catch this money in the act of investing and fall upon it there? I ask the question seriously, though it may be with innocence. It would probably not differ radically from the present tax in effect, but the difference in the clarity of its economic logic would be great. Why not tax all new investments at a uniform rate? The investments might be conveniently defined as new issues of corporation paper, whether the corporations were new or old. I have mentioned such an idea to business men, getting always about the same answer: "It would stop expansion," or, "It would stop progress." But I reply that there will be expansion, and there will be progress, just as surely as there is considerable surplus income on hand and the tax rate does not approximate 100 per cent of it. The business men sometimes alter their objection to the effect that at least the tax would act as a serious brake on expansion and progress; which is exactly the influence I would covet for it.

Of course the tax I am suggesting would fall on investments out of income exclusively; not on an investment out of the proceeds of liquidating another investment; nor on the exchange of one investment for another. It ought certainly to fall on life insurance premiums, so long as they went into the hands of directors who proposed to invest them, though not on premiums that were merely stored away waiting for the time when they should have to be disbursed, if there are insurance companies still doing business of so simple a character.

I have no tax to propose in detail, of course; I am only one of the many amateur economists who used to admire the theoretical beauty of another "single tax," that of Henry George.[6] The tax he proposed was aimed to produce a profound economic effect and not merely to raise the money in the easiest way; it was a tax on the "unearned increment" represented in the valuation of land, and its primary object was to prevent the recurrence of the great business depression of the '70s. It is obvious now that depressions are not due wholly, as he thought, nor even mostly, to the private appropriation of the increase in land values. The inflation of these values and the exaction of exorbitant rents to match them are very much like, respectively, the excessive capitalization of an industry of whatever sort and the taking of a proportionate amount of interest from its total income. A universal tax on new capital investments would hit the inflation of land values whenever it showed in the paper which the land company issued. As a matter of fact, land is a form of capital, and rent is a form of capital earning, and modern economists do not honor these forms with a special set of principles but consider that they fall well under the usual principles of capitalism. If a single tax is desirable which would check the evils of capitalism, and not merely find money for the running expenses of the state, I am suggesting that it might be a comprehensive tax on all new investments and not merely on land alone.

Perhaps even the fund for unemployment insurance would be raised, like other state moneys, from such a source; that is, provided it were already established that the state should obtain this fund at the expense of owners' income. Employees lose their jobs, after all, through the capitalistic ambitions of owners. The additional tax for the insurance of the employees' jobs would fall unerringly on the ambitious owners. I do not suggest that it would be a fitting punishment for them. Capitalistic ambition is not a crime, nor is a political economist a penologist. I only suggest that it would hinder them.

6. Henry George (1839–97), American economist, proposed nationalizing land and taxing it at a high rate. His single-tax plan became the focus of a reform movement in the 1880s.

(6) We come finally, and inevitably, to a remedy for the ills of capitalism which is heroic beyond any comparison with these that have gone before. It is: *Socialism: the abolition of capitalism itself: the substitution of public for private ownership of capital*. The theory had long been well known with us, but it used to be that it was no sooner set up for the purpose of economic discussion than it was knocked down. But that was too soon.

Socialism means to be a thoroughgoing political economy, not just an extension of the state's humanitarian activities as a patchwork upon capitalism. For that reason it is formidable and terrifying. The intention of socialists has something to do with that of labor-unionists, fighting to obtain for wage-earners a larger share of income; and with that of humanitarians, granting special favors to those who have been ousted from the capitalistic economy and are destitute. But it goes a great deal further. It would sweep away the whole system by which wage-earners are at the mercy of the capitalists, and by which they are dispossessed.

Socialism as a cause perhaps enrolls most of its members from the non-capitalists or wage-earners, but it is daily winning recruits from the humanitarians and disinterested neutrals. Here is a paradox: they are humanitarians of such good conscience that they are tired of humanitarianism. It has been told us on good authority that the poor we have with us always; but socialists take the exception that, while the saying may be good for a capitalistic society, it will not be good for theirs. It is this promise which attracts the humanitarians. They resent the fact that they have to make such a frequent and painful business of passing the hat, or even dipping into the public treasury, for the benefit of the poor whom capitalism has expelled from its exclusive society. So much humanitarianism, such a fuss for subscriptions in the name of charity, so many official relief measures, would indicate that the flaw in the operating economy is too grievous altogether; it leaks too badly, and keeps too big a repair squad at work. In some countries the item of relief for the unemployed becomes a dangerous burden on the national budget; it nearly bankrupted Britain. In our country it is a burden on public-spirited people, and on the local governmental units when they will consent to shoulder it. Better, say the humanitarians, just turning into socialists, an economy which would take care of all the citizens in the first place and not have to relieve so much exceptional distress. Evidently the exceptions are becoming so common that they destroy the validity of the rule; let us have a new rule altogether.

The old-time economists to whom capitalism is sacred are visibly scared at the rate conversions are being made to socialism. Some of the finest Americans have gone over. The present breakdown of capitalism is only one out of many, but that is just the trouble; is capitalism going to keep on breaking down at frequent though irregular intervals? Have we not then had enough of capitalism, is it not time to give it up and try something else? It would not be a credit to America if its citizens were all immune to this sort of reasoning; it would argue that we were as hard of heart as of head.

———————

If these are the grounds of socialism, what is its technique? How would the ownership of all the capital by the state prevent destitution and unemployment? How, in particular, would it prevent production getting ahead of purchasing power, so that the producing plant has to reduce its operation, and some of its units exhibit both idle capital and, what is worse, unemployment? It is the practice of overcapitalization which public ownership would principally have to stop.

It would probably stop it, if it did anything. A government running its business with any economic sense would not erect more plant than was needed. The capitalistic motive, which is the desire to create new capital, is a private and competitive motive, wanting in the state. A mere likely danger would rather be, as the critics of socialism have pointed out, that the state would not set aside enough free capital for the proper development of industries. It would run[7] the existing industries as a matter of routine, and stabilize them to the point where they would be incapable of progress, rather than improve them at the cost of new capital investment, or supersede them frequently with expensive establishments of newer model—as Henry Ford tore down a good automobile plant in order to put in its place a better one—or supplement them with new industries producing novel commodities never heard of before. Behind the progress which capitalism has given us is the ceaseless drive of the great quantities of free capital yearning for investment and employing the experimental ingenuity of the ablest engineers whose services can be bought. As between a stability that scarcely permits of change, and a progress that is so rapid it is wasteful and dangerous, if we had to choose between two errors, I might personally prefer the one while somebody else would prefer the other. But the former is the error to which socialism would be liable. The impulse of a democratic government managing the country's business would be to play it safe.

In other words, the rationalization which some sanguine persons call on the capitalists to practice voluntarily is the very thing that a socialistic state would be constantly trying to accomplish. Enough plant to produce for all; extension of the plant when it was imperatively called for; and not one pile of bricks nor one steel girder nor one set-up of machinery beyond. Socialism might be defined as the political economy under which "planning" would be the principal function of government. Capitalism is the political economy in which government knows that planning is the preserve of the private business men, and dare not poach on that preserve.

———

Socialism might not work, it is a desperate gamble. It has never been tried until now, which is the reason why the Russian

7. The original reads, "It would might run." Ransom did not make a correction or indicate a preference for "would" or "might."

experiment is the most thrilling economic adventure ever undertaken. There are many considerations which make us skeptical of the final success of this or any other such experiment. Hundreds of economists have dwelt on them, and I shall not mention them. After all, this is not Russia. It is not even Britain, where because of bad management a government has been turned out which was socialistic in the very timidest sense. This is America, which is anti-socialistic rather more whole-heartedly than it is anything else in the way of its politics, and which has an unequalled capacity for seeing Red upon slight provocation. Americans know all about these considerations, and I will carry no coals to Newcastle.

I shall make only one anti-socialistic remark, and it is not novel.

———————

Capitalism is supported in America by a consideration which is in the strictest sense ethical—it rests on a habit of mind which is native to us racially. Capitalism is a basic principle but not a first principle. It developed naturally out of a principle of private property; and private property has always been to Westerners as a fundamental right, sanctified by our moral code and protected by our jurisprudence. In Aristotle's *Nichomachean Ethics* this right was succinctly defined and justified for the first time in literature, so far as I know. That was a long time ago, but this right has been gaining force and not losing it in the subsequent course of Western history. When you have conceded a man's right to do what he pleases with his property, you cannot object to his lending it out for a charge to his neighbor, and there you have the seed of great fortunes which are strictly private. But when machines are developed, and men assume the right to invest their money in factories equipped for mass-production, you have a much faster accumulation of wealth, you have the essence of our great modern capitalistic enterprises. In theory, you cannot touch the latter right without touching the former one. The reluctance with which we lay hands on any private right is constitutional, all but instinctive, and if we do it for expediency's sake we are not willing to profess it as a principle. It does not suit the moral sense on which we have been acting for so long that it is second nature, if indeed it was not our first nature. It is the nature even of our wage-earners, who have the capitalistic or individualistic psychology much as their employers have it, and who amaze some European observers by their dislike of socialism.

The Russian collectivist experiment has a curious feature. It is conducted by a society not yet industrialized, and almost without experience of the industrial revolution. Everywhere else industrialization has been the work of private capitalism, which is of famous efficiency for the job, and only where the job is far advanced would the observer expect to see society calling off its private owners in order to consolidate and maintain their conquests. The Russian program is engineered by men who have admired the industrial technique of private capitalism but hated the economic evils that beset its late stages; and they intend first to collectivize Russia, and then to industrialize it. It is a big undertaking.

But probably it is not so big an undertaking as that which a collectivist program offers to a country already fully industrialized, but habituated to private ownership and investment psychology.

———————

Socialism is a hard alternative to capitalism. Shall we go on with our old irrational capitalism, and continue to suffer under the old abuses, though we thoroughly disrespect it, and are convinced all the time that it will never cease to commit its abuses as long as it lives? Or shall we rationalize it, which means that we shall forcibly appropriate the capital and try to run it in the public interest, though that is an undertaking both alien to our temperament and dubious in its prospect of success? Before this dilemma our most spirited citizens are in agonies of dismay.

But perhaps it is not exactly necessary to choose definitively, as if by the crossing of a ballot, between the two economies, the violent irresponsible one and the dull tyrannical one. There is an economy which is neither the one nor the other, and it can still be practiced. It is agrarianism; neglected, but recoverable; about which there is more to say presently. Its recovery would open a grand new world to many people now suffering, whether materially or temperamentally, under the hard conditions of capitalism; and an economy could scarcely be further spiritually from socialism. We have not canvassed our situation thoroughly if we fail to attend to that possibility. We have scarcely been in a position to appreciate its excellencies until now, when we have had sad experience of capitalism, and contemplate with mixed feelings the stealthy approach of a rescuer who is only socialism.

Chapter 4

THE AMPHIBIAN FARMER

Our industries are overdeveloped and overproductive. From the investors' point of view, they are not yielding a satisfactory return on capital, nor is the investment even a safe one; and from the wage-earners' point of view, they are largely at a standstill, having withdrawn much of the employment they undertook to furnish and turned the unemployed out upon the world by the million.

That is the situation for which I suggest relief through a return to agriculture. But at first sight agriculture looks like the most unlikely industry for this purpose on the whole list. Let us look at its present status.

Of all the industries that are suffering today, farming is notorious in having a complaint that is peculiarly deep-seated or chronic rather than periodic or acute. Since the war it has not had good years and bad years, but only bad ones. And all this time it has been crying for relief, loudly as well as constantly. It does not seem to go up and down as if it were fully responsive to the business cycle. It may be a little less down when the other industries are flourishing and keeping all their employees on the payroll, where they are in a position to buy farm products; but not much less. It is generally agreed by economists all over the world that the price of primary products, especially farm products, is too low at the present; the world's concern over this fact is not entirely altruistic but wishful that the farmer, by receiving better prices, might buy more freely from the other producers. But when were the prices of farm products high enough to make the rewards of farming proportionate to those of the other industries? They have not reached that figure in our time.

The farm business never quite takes the cure that industries must ordinarily and automatically take for hard times: the abandonment of excess capital plant and reorganization on a reduced scale of production. Though some farmers are willing to abandon their farms, there are never nearly enough of them doing it to restore prosperity to those that are left. Evidently the farmers lead charmed lives, economically, or they could not survive in such large numbers in so miserable an industry. How do they manage it? This is a fascinating question, and even the simple asking of it suggests that farming is no ordinary industry.

But there is not room to doubt that its malady is a perfectly trite one: overcapitalization: a capital plant that is bigger than it needs to be and has more personnel depending on it than it can support: overproduction: too many farms and too many farmers. The plant of this industry is the total acreage of land from which come the farm products to be sold on the market. It is evidently excessive. Land is a form of productive capital which does not have to be erected by builders; it is natural; it is there already and needs only be appropriated. There is no industry which it is so easy to capitalize, or put into active production, as one whose plant consists in a natural resource which is plentiful. Farm land is one such resource, but others are oil, coal, timber, and the like; all of which at one time or another have given rise to industries which have suffered from overproduction. It is easy to ask the owners not to put such resources into production all at once; yet there is the plant, ready-made and waiting; and here are the owners, probably owning nothing else and obliged to defend their economic existence by making such use of this capital as they can; or at least willing to undertake something else if this did not promise them more income. The farm owners are far from operating their immense plant at its maximum capacity. They talk about holding back—each one probably talking mostly for the benefit of the other owners—

and they actually perform something in this line, but even so their produce nearly every season destroys its market with its own superfluity.

The continental area of the United States is about 1,900,000,000 acres, of which nearly half is capable of some sort of cultivation. But only something over 300,000,000 acres is actually under cultivation. It is as if our total population consisted in families of five persons each, and every family had a property of 75 acres, of which it found it necessary to farm only about a dozen acres; though that would be a misleading statement if it were supposed to describe the actual distribution of land or the actual occupation of the people. Actually, the farming is done by a class of professional farmers who are distinctly a minority of the population, but who hold the arable land and make it productive for the sustenance of all. In that capacity it is only too productive. A much-quoted estimate of the farm land and farm production in America declares that, of the land actually under cultivation, which is the cream of the land capable of cultivation, but by no means all of it, 40 percent is "marginal." We are to understand from this term that 40 percent of the land was worth nothing or less than nothing as an investment purchase, since the sale of its produce did not yield anything in the way of interest on a capital valuation. The situation must be really worse than that, when we stop to consider that much of the other 60 percent is not perfectly tilled and could be made more productive, and that much tillable land is not tilled at all. What then is the actual excess of American farm land? One guess is about as good as another here where nobody knows. A rather conservative one that I have heard is more than 50 percent; it would not take half the land resources of this country, if it were farmed with a will, and with fair scientific efficiency, to supply the whole available market with farm products.

What can the state do for farming? I mean, of course, short of taking over the farms, along with all the other forms of capital, and operating them in somewhat the manner adopted by the Soviet government. Much as I like farming as a profession, and respect the farmers, I am obliged to make the answer that is almost universally made by our political economists: The state can do little or nothing for farming as an industry. Is the state to subsidize farming, increase its revenues by arbitrary gift, make it profitable for all the marginal farmers as it is not profitable in the ordinary course of events? If the state were going to help any industry at the expense of the others, it might well be the one that was the poorest; except that in this case the poorest is also the largest. The state can hardly do it; must not, in the interest of its impartial position; and cannot, in the sense that any relief which would be effective would probably be ruinous to the community of industries, and eventually to the state itself.

Whatever the state might do, it could not avoid the obvious fact that the land in this country is excessive, when regarded as the capital of a productive industry. The more profitable the farming of this land became under a plan of state assistance, the larger it might expect the volume of its production to grow; and to promise the profitable disposal of an indefinitely increasing surplus in the largest of all the industries would be to offer to a privileged industry a bonus which it would soon become impossible for a state to pay.

And yet a sort of subsidy on a modest scale has just been actually tried. The Farm Board that has been maintained by the United States government for several years was a hopeless experiment from the beginning. It proposed to control the market for certain farm products and keep up prices. It was going to buy wheat and cotton whenever the prices were off in order to stimulate the market, and it was not going to sell until the market could stand it. The Farm Board has done a great deal of buying, subject to the limitation of its operating funds, but it has not dared to do much more than talk about selling. Each time it has started to sell, the current prices were threatened, and the outcry arising from the farmers was sufficient to frighten the Board from its course. The failure of this project has been complete. But failure was apparent in advance to political economists; it seemed to be apparent also to the realistic Republican officials who reluctantly put the measure of into operation. The best that can be said of this failure is that it has been a salutary one, for it has defined the situation for many who could not define it for themselves. The measure was favored on the innocent assumption that the over-production with which it proposed to deal was slight, or was temporary, or was both. The attempt to hold the surplus of wheat and cotton for a better market broke down because the surplus is both large and constant. But even if it had not been already, the prospect of a good price for wheat and cotton would immediately have turned the farmers to the raising of these preferred crops and made a regular surplus inevitable. You cannot guarantee income to any free industry in these days without speeding up its over-capitalization.

Nevertheless the state has done a great deal for American farmers, by and large—much more than it has done for any other class of producers. For one thing, it has continually exerted itself to get new lands for them to work, by purchase, conquest, draining, irrigation, and sanitation. Our national parties used to boast of this when they recounted the glories of their administrations, and even I can remember how a plank in this style went regularly into the official party platforms. They do not boast of it so much now, because it is seen that new lands mean new capital for production, and the industry is already overproducing. New lands are fine for their private owners, who had no lands or inferior lands before, but they are not so good for the general economy of the industry.

The state has also done a special and very handsome service to the farmer by instructing him how to conduct his business efficiently. The Department of Agriculture has been laboring for him many years, while the vaguely analogous Department of Commerce and Labor has been laboring for all the other industrialists only since the Roosevelt administration. The 48 Experiment Stations, co-operating with the local governments of the States, have brought the lessons of scientific efficiency right to the farmer's door.

But science in coming to the American farms has on the whole had a dismal effect; it has caused them to produce more goods per acre, to increase the total volume of farm products, and to throw more and more farm lands over the margin into the category of the unprofitable forms of capital. Scientific farming is like scientific management, it is like the installation of labor-saving machinery— very valuable for the private farmer, and indeed indispensable if he would stand up under the competition, but of doubtful benefit to the industry as a whole. Machines and technical improvements reduce the capital and labor requirements in an industry, as they are meant to do, but incidentally, under our modern American conditions, they overcapitalize the industry and evict its laborers.

The farming industry is not more rational than other industries but, if anything, less rational. The individual farmer must increase his production as hard as he can if he expects to get a return on his land, and the lower the current price per bushel, the more bushels he must make per acre. But this is the reasoning not of one farmer but of all farmers, and a great surplus of farm produce is the consequence. The aggregate of all the sound private economies does not make a sound political economy. That is the rock on which capitalism threatens to founder, and the farming industry is its most jagged promontory.

———————

But if scientific management for the private farmer does not improve the condition of the industry as a whole, the extension of scientific management which is known as rationalization will not do it either. Rationalization for the farmers takes the form of cooperative organizations whose purpose is to restrict the production through agreement, and also to hold back the products from sale until the market is favorable. Neither of these objects can quite be accomplished. The government's farm experts plead with the farmers to reduce their acreage. But what do they expect the farmers to do with their acres but farm them? Behind the marginal acres are the marginal owners, whose capital happens to be land,

and who must make this land produce if they expect to have any use of their ownership.

The futility of schemes of rationalization in any economic society founded on free individualism had a perfect demonstration last summer in the abortive movement to persuade cotton farmers to destroy or stop production in order to force the cotton market to use up the surplus on hand and then bid high for more. The Farm Board came out with the radical proposal that the farmers plow up one row in every three so that the total crop would be reduced by 5,000,000 bales. The Governors of the Southern States were canvassed with varying results. Some did not approve of sabotage on principle; some thought it could not be unanimously and therefore effectively carried out; some made other proposals of their own. The most vigorous of these was that of Governor Long of Louisiana, who went before his Legislature to ask for a bill prohibiting the raising of cotton in the State during 1932, provided the Legislatures of other States whose cotton production aggregated three-fourths of the total crop passed bills to the same effect.[1] His own Legislature accommodated him but no other. The Governor and the Legislature of Texas, a State with far more at stake in cotton than any other, emphatically rejected the plan, and it went no further.[2] It had probably gone too far already. Its economics were doubtful. You must not deprive your citizens of the occupation they have unless you furnish them with some other. The cotton farmers thought they could not go without their cotton money for a whole year, any more than strikers can leave work and go without wages for that period, or owners in any industry can stop their plants and go without income. Or was there something special in their condition as farmers which might have made them indifferent to their crop-money as ordinary industrialists can never be indifferent to their usual source of income? This question was hardly raised. At most I observed the suggestion that the cotton farmers could devote their land to raising truck for the

1. Huey Long, governor of Louisiana from 1928 to 1932.
2. Ross Sterling, governor of Texas from 1931 to 1933.

market, or other marketable products, in the meantime. But this ignored the fact that overproduction in farmstuffs is sweeping and universal; there was no kind of market production that could have borne the accession of the cotton farmers for even a year's time. The plan of a cotton holiday therefore broke down. The farmers wanted their money, even if it was less than they felt entitled to.

———————

But now let us go back to a question that suggested itself about the farmers above. What is the source of the farmer's strength that permits him to continue in an unprofitable industry? (For some farmers do; enough to make the industry exceptional and require an explanation from economists.) How can he afford to stay on the land when it makes him such a miserable income? Why is there never a single great crash in this large and impossible industry that will force a scaling down of the capital plant and a re-organization on a lower and properer basis?

These are important questions, though it is evident that many economists never ask them nor answer them. If they did, they would see at once that a farmer is like no other capitalist. He is worse off in one respect, but in another respect he has an incalculable advantage.

This is the advantage: Economically, he is an amphibian, for he can live in either of the two elements and, when one betrays him, he needs only to turn to the other. A farmer is never forced to quit his farm merely because it brings him a low money income, or even practically no income at all. That is only one of his economies wherein he sustains life on a money income; but it is always possible for him to try another economy and sustain life on a non-monetary basis.

Like a creature that can live in the sea or on the land, the farmer may make money and buy his necessities, or he can acquire his necessities directly without money and without exchange. The economy of modern capitalism, whose every good thing comes through money, is his sea element. The primitive, pioneering, old-fashioned agrarian economy, where his goods are wrested directly from nature and consumed on the premises, are his land element. I waste no tears on the poor farmer, who as a general thing makes no great success of making money today. I observe that even in this unimpressive condition he is not done for, he continues to farm just the same as if he were succeeding brilliantly. And perhaps he hardly knows, in terms of economic theory, how he does it. But he does it simply by making with his own hands what he cannot find the money to buy. As Stuart Chase says, when the books will not balance he has only to throw them out the window and go pick some peas.[3]

We shall have to study these two economies, and we must name them. I should think the best terms are as I have given them: the agrarian economy, and the capitalistic. The latter is necessarily the money economy, the ordinary modern economy. The agrarian economy is a direct subsistence economy. The strict theoretical economist may insist that the farmer's land is a capital even if he only takes his food from it, and that the food should be classified as the income it produces whether it be sold on the market or not. But capital and income, after all, are terms which came in with the growth of money, and in this last usage they are being referred far back and imposed upon a more elementary economy for only technical reasons. Capitalism is an economy of investments measurable by money, and of returns also measurable by money. Agrarianism is an economy in which money plays a subordinate and occasional part, or into which it even fails to enter.

———————

My elders tell me of a saying in my section which their elders used to repeat to them when they were young; it was probably widespread. It was for the benefit of the wise young men of the community when they began to think too much of farming in terms of money: "If you try to make money on the farm, you will go broke; but if you try to make a good living on the farm, you will make money." These old men were prophets.

3. Stuart Chase (1888–1985), American economist and adviser to Franklin D. Roosevelt credited with coining "New Deal."

For, something like a generation or two ago, the American farmer, who was making a good living for himself on the agrarian plan, became too much impressed with the theory of the capitalistic economy, under which so many fabulous fortunes were being made, and decided to apply it to farming. Under this theory the farmer was to sell his whole labor, and the whole use of his capital, for money; then he was to take the money and buy whatever he needed with it. The theory had done well indeed in American industry, and under it was being reared the magnificent structure of American capitalism, with prosperity abounding at least periodically for nearly everybody. A man devoting himself and his wealth to the textiles, or to steel, or to the building trades, or to railroads, might ordinarily expect to get good money income, and with it go out and buy profusely of the commodities he wanted. He bought his house and lot, his furniture, his food and clothing, his comforts, and possibly the services of a janitor, a landscape gardener, and a cook.

But that was all he could do. The steel maker makes steel, or at least some part of it, but he cannot eat steel, nor clothe himself with it, nor shelter under it from the rain; there being no direct connection between his own act of manufacture and what he needs in order to live. The farmer, on the other hand, is engaged in producing vegetables, meats, tobacco, fibres, timber— precisely the raw materials of the staples of living, and some of them ready for immediate consumption. The steel man *must* get money. The farmer *may* get money if he likes; but he may also prefer to provide himself with his necessities with hardly the exchange of a dollar. Nobody else in the whole economic society is in that position.

More usually, of course, and ever since the frontier stages in every part of this country, the farmer had made much of his own living with his hands and then supplemented it with the purchases he has made with money; he has rarely been innocent of all money transactions, though professionally he is engaged in producing most of the means of life. The farmer in his better days used to produce some choice foods for his own table. He provided himself with eggs, milk, butter; he made his own supply of vegetables, cereals, fruits, honey, and syrups, canned foods. He enjoyed a fair assortment of fresh meats and poultry, and he cured his own hams, which, if they were of the general description of Virginia hams, were better than anything the packing houses had to sell him. He could have grass on his lawn, trees, flowers, in far greater quantity than the average city dweller, and as fine as he cared to make them. He was very largely his own carpenter, keeping his dwelling, his outhouses and fences in decent repair, and knowing the uses of paint and whitewash. He let the womenfolk of his family make the cloth and the clothing, at one period; though after he came well within range of the industrial revolution of the Nineteenth Century he preferred to buy these articles on the market, and he could buy them without compromising too deeply his self-sufficient economy. For he made a good deal of money on the side. He made his own living first and then he attended to his money crops.

But the American farmer abandoned this impregnable position, and has been trying with all his might to bring the capitalistic economy to the farm. He went in for money-making. He tried to do mass-production in specialized money crops, on such a scale as he could. He aimed both at volume and at economy of production, because this was the formula of successful capitalism. And it is true that some of the large Western farmers with very fine level land, and some smart farmers everywhere, have had considerable success, though hardly the success they looked for—hardly the success that their still smarter cousins were having in other industries. Generally, the farmer has been bitterly disillusioned. He is as weak and underprivileged trying to play the money game as he was strong and comfortable sticking to his ancient agrarian economy. The land-owner has got a scanty money return on his investment; about as often as not he has incurred a loss, and mortgaged his lands to the local banker, or the government, or the insurance company. The farm hand has been consistently unable to get wages equal to those paid at the mills. The collective unanimity with which the farmers have devoted themselves to producing almost exclusively for the market has brought about an overproduction which seems to be incurable. There is no money in producing what everybody else is producing.

And in the meantime the farmer has gradually forgotten the solid comforts which once made him envied. He has been too intent on his money-cropping to have strength or imagination left over for keeping up his orchard, for tending his lawn and shrubs, and even for repairing his tumbledown habitation. He thought he could pay to have these things done for him, and when it proved that he was mistaken he forgot that he could do them himself. His garden is often a way of speaking more than anything else, and sometimes it does not exist at all. The Virginia hams and smoked sausages are becoming extinct on the face of the earth, while the Southern farmers add always a little more to the overproduction of apples, peaches, corn, cotton, and tobacco, and the farmers of other sections do something similar. The farmer expected that with the handsome revenues derived from his sales he could furnish out his table in satisfactory style, like the city man's table. He has been able to do nothing of the sort. Many farmers today are selling the butter-fat produced by their cows to the canned-milk plants in order to buy oleomargarine for their tables. A Kansas man told me last year that the farmers of his State who had been selling all their eggs and chickens were stopped when the bottom dropped out of the market; but that since then, ironically enough, they had been living rather better than before because they had had to assimilate these items to their own diet.

There still exist some exceptional farmers who insist on making themselves a good living first, and then what money they can; I know them. They do not find it physically harder to do this than it was thirty years ago, but easier; for the technique has improved in every department of farming. And sometimes, even in recent years, there have come to this country patriarchal colonies of German, Swiss, or Eastern European farmers, untutored in the great capitalistic economy, who have settled down on some tract of mediocre land, worked out their titles to it by heroic labors, and finally converted a wilderness into a garden where they live with an air of thrifty prosperity that refreshes the eye of the discouraged traveler.

But it is more usual in my section to find along the roadside a fairly unbroken succession of farm places that bear the marks of decay and even squalor. Their able-bodied population is either hustling about its money-making chores or else it is sitting down in utter discouragement. These people are whipped; they know it and they show it. Enough time has elapsed since the money idea came to the farm for the present generation of farmers to have nearly lost their sense of living by any other economy. The amphibian is about to forget his primary element, he is suffering under the strange delusion that he must continue to wallow painfully in the element he is in.

———————

What solution therefore will a political economist, one who has not acquired his theory at the cost of his common sense, offer for the farm problem? He will offer none at all for the problem of farming as a modern industry. He will be honest enough to tell the farmers who farm with this point of view that they must take their medicine. There is no hope for this industry until it is decapitalized and reduced in its personnel. But no political economist can begin to tell it just how it may eliminate its marginal capital and marginal capitalists with this object in view. That is a surgical operation on a grand scale, and surgery is not being practiced in this country on that scale.

Nevertheless to the individual farmer he has something to say, and chiefly this: Let him remember his amphibianism. The individual farmer's problem is extremely easy of solution as compared with that of the individual steel man, textile man, oil man, builder, or merchant. This latter man may yet be completely ruined, he may become an object of the state's charity, or even perish. But the farmer is invulnerable and immortal. His dependence in the last resort is upon the easy bounty of nature. The other's dependence is upon the working of an economy which is the mechanical aggregate of many private transactions, with involutions that are sometimes crazy and sometimes destructive.

It is unfortunate that our modern political economists are so entirely committed to the capitalistic or money economy. They come out of educational institutions that have no contact with any genuine agrarian economy, and write books out of cities that are perfectly insulated from it. Their eye is on Pittsburgh, New York, Detroit, Akron; their ear is adapted to the utterances of manufacturers, labor unionists, travelling salesmen, Chambers of Commerce, and clamorous money-farmers. And yet there is an agrarian economy which barely survives here and there, an agrarian theory which is just as practicable today as ever, and an agrarian tradition which is recoverable. Agrarianism is known in parts of the South if not at the publishing centers of the economists. It lingers, or a little of its fragrance lingers, in the upper Western reaches of the Mississippi Valley. It is continually being imported by humble Europeans, who generally forget it in the following generation. It needs devoted political economists to come to its support. If these will speak out for it, they will soon be echoed by the politicians, the educators, the editors, the preachers, and all the community leaders, and perhaps again an uncommercial breed of farmers will come into existence.

———————

The political economists might, as a matter of theory, announce quite flatly that agrarianism is the only sound policy for American farmers today, unless some 40 per cent of them will kindly commit euthanasia and remove themselves from the economic scene. Then, on the technical side, they should change the character of the instruction that farmers of our generation have been receiving. What the farmers have been getting from the agricultural experts of the schools and experiment stations is the lesson of increased productivity. This has reference primarily to volume of production per unit of land and labor. Unfortunately for the farmers as a class, it has been only too well learned, and its effect has been to send to market a greater total volume of products and make it more difficult for famers to survive. If the farmers and the political economists were so wedded to the money economy, it would have been better if the former, advised by the latter, had tried for a stationary productivity or a decreased productivity; then they all might have retained their place in the economic society; whereas by becoming greater producers they have destroyed themselves. But at any rate, if they are to renounce their exclusive occupation with the money economy, they will need a quite different technical instruction.

The technique which leads the farmer to provide himself with expensive equipment and launch into the large-scale production of one or two money crops is not the technique by which he will sustain himself as an agrarian. His land will have to be put to many uses and he will have to be a man of many occupations. He should practice each one as efficiently as he can, but he must not expect to develop the same productivity in any one as he might if he devoted himself exclusively to it. This consideration is a blow at the modern ideal of maximum efficiency in the current meaning of that term; the agrarian economy must develop its own kind of maximum efficiency, which is a different kind.

The problem of the agricultural school if it should attempt to teach agrarian farming, or farming as a whole, would be rather like that of the liberal college in one respect: when so many branches are taught by enthusiastic specialists, each one naively assuming that the pupils are exclusively interested in his branch, the problem is to co-ordinate or balance these specialties for the benefit of the man who proposes to use them all at once. The procedures taught by the specialists are counsels of perfection which are scarcely capable of practice by the all-round farmer. The self-sufficient farm is an undertaking in balance and correlation. Two generations ago this kind of farming still had a living tradition to go by. The father handed down the farm to the son; the farm was already successfully going, and the son was already familiar with its formula; if he shifted the balance among its various activities he did it cautiously and empirically. The formula is pretty well lost now, and has to be recovered; in part by the empirical farmer, in part by his economic advisor.

This last-named has grown too used to telling the farmer, on the productive side, how to specialize on the given kind of production for the market; and on the economic side, how to study the market, decide what specialty it will pay best to go in for, and keep books.

The really high-powered economist, or super-economist, has had his head full of the widest and most abstract considerations of world-markets and world-problems, and he has indulged in grandiose but fairly impracticable schemes. Such economists are the "planners." When they hold a meeting to plan for the agricultural industry, they are apt to decide that the marginal land should be put into forest, that marginal owners and hired hands should be "absorbed into other industries," that a new market for farm products must be developed in China, and by all means that new surveys and studies must be made at once and got ready for the next meeting. These pretty schemes have no sort of meaning for actual dirt-farmers, and there is probably no power on earth capable of putting them into effect this side of Russia. Such agricultural economists must come down to the ground.

The self-sufficient farm, which must often be a one-family one and a small one at that, may seem to offer insufficient opportunity for the economists to spread themselves and exercise their talents; it is a study in little business, not in big business. But its economic problems are difficult all the same.

———————

It takes brawn and hard work to do any farming at all, and it takes brains in addition to run the self-sufficient farm. It is not so much that the farmer has a lot of difficult chores to do, though that is the fact. If the city man imagines that farming is an unskilled occupation, let him go out and see if he can plow a straight furrow, or put the stock into the stable and feed them, or milk a cow, or shock the oats after the binder has gone through, or cut down a tree and convert it into cords of piled stovewood. A single all-around farmer must have twenty of thirty different skills. But these are the A, B, C's of farming; out of them the farmer must construct a rational language, which is the economy of agrarianism.

The economic questions that arise are such as the following. The question of the garden, one of the simplest; how large a garden, how much to each vegetable, how much to allow for summer canning. Similarly as to fruits. As for dairy products, how many cows to keep. As for meats, how much poultry, how many beeves (if any) and hogs, how much pork to cure for winter. How many head of work-stock. But, for all the livestock, the question of food supply, in pasturage, grain, hay; and the question of breeding. Questions of housing, for man and beast; how much capital outlay is justified. Questions of labor supply; if outside labor, whether hired labor or tenant labor; and the question of food and housing for the latter. As for tools, the difficult question whether to buy the best tools or avoid so much capital outlay. Then, for the one source of revenue to meet capital and current expenditures in money, the question of what market production to undertake, how much land, equipment, and labor to invest in it. These are some of the major questions. Fortunately they do not all have to be settled at once, and fortunately they do not all have to be settled right the first time. No other business is so elastic in its formula, and none is so forgiving of mistakes—except of the one mistake of getting deeply involved in debt.

It is safe to say that few of the highly specialized businesses in the productive community of capitalism face such a complex of problems as this. Probably the same intelligence which would run a small factory or an ordinary merchandising establishment would also run a farm on the capitalistic basis, allowing even for "diversification" in the crops. It is doubtful if it would run a self-sufficient farm. The latter presents a greater variety of factors which have to be organized, and a looser play in the organization which has to be taken into account by the judgment. One reason why the appeals to something perennial in the generations of men is because it offers expression to Man Thinking as well as to Man Laboring.[4] Business houses and money-farms require some thinking, but after all these are able to keep accurate books on their transactions; and book-keeping will not do for the agrarian farmer. The items with which he deals are concrete and difficult, not abstract and precise sums of money.

4. There is no handwritten correction to "the appeals" in this sentence. The meaning is clearer if rendered thus: "One reason why *it* [or *this*] appeals to something perennial in the generations of men is because it offers expression to Man Thinking as well as to Man Laboring."

But I indicated that agriculture was not only a profession which might be made good for those already practicing it—a thing it has not been within our time—but one so hospitable that it might absorb some of the present excess of personnel throughout our economic order.

I have in mind an "agrarian movement" rather formidable in its proportions. Not only will it denote a shift of standards on the part of the present farmers. If it becomes orthodox in theory, and begins to justify itself in practice, inevitably much of the swollen personnel of industry will find its way back to the land. Not, of course, for the purpose of another money-making venture, for an agrarian movement of that sort would be a movement from the frying-pan into the fire; but for the purpose of practicing a genuine agrarianism, which is first of all, and as largely as practicable, a private economy of self-subsistence. Discouraged townsmen will be glad to go to the farm when they are made familiar with its new, yet immemorial, possibilities. They will be starting out again on the land much as their pioneer forefathers did. They will not expect money-wealth from it, but they will expect that after some initial hardship they will achieve a comfortable standard of living, which is more than any other occupation in America can promise them at the moment.

It can just barely be said that there are signs of an agrarian movement in this double sense: a new economic practice for the existing farmers; a return to the land on the part of the townsmen.

A succession of bad years for the cotton growers—bad for the growers in the sense that they were good for the cotton—has determined many Southern farmers not to be caught again without food in the cellar though very likely they may be caught again without money in the bank. Even the most incompetent and underprivileged of these farmers, who are the tenants, are beginning to reform. Something occurs to them at least which they had tried to forget: that a garden is as good a place as a store to get vegetables from, a flock of chickens furnishes real eggs and meat, and a cow gives milk and butter as well as a dairy. Their landlords, by a change of head if not of heart, are helping them to recall it, having found it too expensive to keep them on the books of the company store when their earnings are not high enough to stand the necessary deductions. (It seems incredible that great numbers of Southern farmers, both small owners and tenants, should have abandoned their home-made diet, but it is true.) The canning of summer vegetables and fruits has again become popular in remote and poverty-stricken communities, encouraged by the Red Cross, which has had experience of more costly ways of relieving famine. And I think I have observed a brightening up of farm properties, as if the owners had decided they would be there for some time and had as well make the best of it.

On the part of the townsfolk there is a fresh interest in the questions of where there is land available for early occupation and what its price is. The migration from country to town, which has been going on steadily in this nation for a hundred years, is beginning to stop and even to reverse itself. The census of 1930 showed that the large towns had continued to gain during the decade but that the small towns were often losing, and losing to the surrounding country as well as to the large towns. In the two years since, this tendency has been heavily accented. The countrymen are staying in the country because, if for no other reason, they have nowhere to go. The Chambers of Commerce were very glad to see them come to town a few years ago, for they swelled the population, and it was expected that if they did not exactly prove an ornament to the town, they would at least be able to support themselves with employment at the new factory which the Chamber's Secretary had enticed into the community. But some of the recent growth of the towns has been found to have not been worth the growing-pains; the industries which supported it have collapsed and the ex-farmers are now on the charity of the town. The new decade will be a bad one for Chambers of Commerce, who will probably have to pay in philanthropy for some of their excessive labors of the last decade. It will not be surprising if some Chambers do not develop land schemes to dispose of the superfluous population for which they are responsible. It would certainly please many of the derelict ex-farmers—especially if they heard there was now on trial a new idea of farming by which they might do better than before.

American opinion is evidently very sensitive at this moment to the deficiencies in its economy. Is it land-conscious? Astonishing news reaches me through a full-page article submitted to a London daily from "Our Own American Correspondent." It tells of a change of attitude on the part of the American public which I should define as going in the direction of agrarian. The housewives have abandoned the cafeteria and gone back into the kitchen, the grocery shops decline because the family garden has come into an importance it has not had since war days, the farmers propose to make themselves a living even if the market for their crops breaks completely down, and public speakers advise that every household become as complete a domestic economy as it can—an *oikonomike* in the original Greek sense.[5] But I distrust this news. I think it is largely the fabrication of a European who still knows of an old reliable kind of economy which Americans considered that they had outgrown, and then lost sight of.

I note also, in the huge special American number of a French periodical, lavishly illustrated, an article about America strangely exceptional in a context devoted to the usual story of American skyscrapers, big business, and lavish expenditures. Its title might be rendered, "Another Side of America," and it is written by Pierre de Lanux about no other subject than the agrarian South, where there is an attempt being made to save the old tradition of self-sufficient country households in defiance of the sweep of industrialization.[6] This is evidently another European comment, perhaps a little in advance of the fact. M. de Lanux as a friend and a Frenchman would like to see an agrarian revival which would save to America a certain European and eminently French quality which is vanishing.

---

5. From the Greek *oikos*, "house"; Ransom's original reads: "every household become as complete *as* domestic economy as it can" (italics added).

6. Pierre Combret de Lanux (1887–1955), French writer and diplomat, author of *Young France and New America* (1917).

I should not dare to say that an agrarian movement is under way though the times are ripe for it. It waits mostly upon the endorsement of the economists, who in our day and generation occupy the place of the prophets. Under their direction an agrarian movement in America would be much easier and quicker of effect than was the Danish national and agricultural revival which took half a century, or the Irish revival, which on its agricultural side under the leadership of Plunkett took a little less.[7] Plunkett had to address fifty meetings of unhappy Irishmen before he could found his first co-operative society! Americans, who are both suggestible and energetic, would work faster than that.[8]

———————

But suburbanization, which has been proceeding rapidly in America since the spread of motor cars, has little to do with agrarianism. People who can afford it tend increasingly to go to the country to live, but are careful to live in easy reach of the city, where their occupation lies. The showy country homes of rich people do not betoken agrarian households and have no more significance economically than the city homes of the same class. Their inhabitants do, however, indicate a certain taste for the country; they have at least the picnic view of nature if they do not love nature; they can afford to have any attitude towards her they like, for they do not rely upon her economically in the least.

Nor is there much agrarianism in a recent tendency on the part of industries to get away from the crowded industrial areas and

7. Denmark's cooperative farms were much admired by American progressives after World War I. Daniel T. Rogers writes, "The American-Scandinavian Foundation, organized to promote mutual exchanges between the Scandinavian countries and the United States, granted special traveling fellowships for the study of Danish cooperative agriculture, Danish industrial organization, and the Danish folk high schools." See Rogers, *Atlantic Crossings: Social Politics in a Progressive Age* (Cambridge, MA: Harvard, 1998), 355.

8. Sir Horace Curzon Plunkett (1854–1952), English-born agricultural reformer, founder of the Irish Agricultural Organisation Society (1894), and agricultural advisor to the United States.

erect their plants in the small towns or in the country; this centrifugal tendency is the consequence of new facilities of power transmission, but indicates no attitude of any sort toward the land.

But in those factory colonies located in the country, and in the unpretentious homes of the small towns, there may be people not agrarian by occupation, but attempting to strike some items off the family budget by such elementary home enterprises as chicken-yards, gardens, and fruit trees. These enterprises, unless it is very recently, have been steadily losing ground, and for good economic reasons. A town man both occupied and preoccupied with his business hardly has time for his garden and if he hires a man to tend it for him it is a luxury rather than an economy; the professionals who raise truck on a large scale can sell him his garden products cheaper than he can have them raised in his own garden. He had better put the plot into flowers and call it pleasure rather than utility. But the laboring man may make a real contribution to his expenses by having a garden, if he has labor-energy left over from his regular employment to do the gardening himself. That is the agrarian idea, though it has little room to grow.

A business man of my acquaintance, reared in the country, moved from the city into a suburban place of several acres and tried some home-made production, justifying it on the ground of economy as well as taste. His wife and children wanted to tend to the cows, the fowls, and the hogs, and he hired a man to help the boys with the garden. But now the projects have all fallen through, except the garden, which is reduced in scale. It appeared that the feed consumed by the beasts cost as much as the finished products would have cost. This little bit of agrarianism failed because it was not on the right scale. The feed meant a money outlay to the suburbanite, but on the self-sufficient farm, however small, it would have been home-made too. I should not imagine that suburban or half-way experiments in agrarianism can succeed, though they should hardly be allowed to discount the prospects of real agrarianism.

Ralph Borsodi in his book, *This Ugly Civilization*, makes many good recommendations to people who have the time and want to save some money by producing some things at home.[9] But he is not really proposing an agrarian reform, or anything like it. Agrarianism, if it is to mean much, must be a bold movement advocated in a big way.

None of these little movements, and not all of them put together, will amount to an agrarian revival. At the best they are psychological straws showing how the wind of temperament blows. They indicate that people temperamentally still like to supply their own wants if they can, to make complete things with their hands, to get their fingers into the soil. They are spiritually important and economically insignificant.

———

Mr. Henry Ford's views are economically more important, though they are anti-agrarian views. As an indefatigable amateur economist he has expressed himself about the farm problem, as all economists do sooner or later, and his proposition is that the farmers may expect to prosper when they not only raise their crops in the summer but work in factories in the winter. It is a proposition which has at least the merits of novelty and neatness, and I shall compare it briefly with the agrarian proposal.

It implies in the first place that a farmer's crops do not give him a year-round occupation, and do not afford him a sufficient income. Mr. Ford is thinking entirely of money farmers, and for farmers of that kind both points may be granted, the latter one the less grudgingly. He would supplement this occupation with industrial occupation in the hope that by having alternating occupations the farmer could be fully occupied and in receipt of an appropriate income.

The proposal that farmers go agrarian contains a similar implication. They do their money crops very well indeed, and it is hard

9. Ralph Borsodi, *This Ugly Civilization* (New York: Simon & Schuster, 1929); Borsodi (1886–1977) was an American agrarian writer.

work while it lasts, but it leaves them with insufficient income to go through the winter on. But if the farmer does not stop with his money crop, or does not even start there, but produces in all events whatever he can for his own consumption, winter consumption included—if he is his own carpenter, painter, roadmaker, forester, meatpacker, woodcutter, gardener, landscape gardener, nurseryman, dairyman, poulterer, and handyman—then he has a fair-sized man's job on his hands which will occupy him sufficiently at all seasons. His hard work will come in the spring and summer, but if his work slackens after that, no confirmed lover of nature will begrudge him a little leisure for hunting, fishing, and plain country meditation. Though a factory occupation might bring in a revenue quite equal or superior to buying in the services which he is supplying with his own hands directly, it would present the objection that it would be altogether different from his normal occupation and possibly distasteful. He would be half a farmer and half an industrialist, which would seem to tend to an unnatural disintegration of his personality.

But the conclusive argument against the Ford farm plan is that it would not relieve but aggravate the general economic situation, of which the distressing feature is unemployment due to overproduction, and that under existing circumstances it is impossible. In what factories would the farmers labor? Hardly in the Ford factories, for Mr. Ford is periodically obliged, quite like other owners, to lay off a great many of his own men, who came to him not for a season but for full-time employment. An agrarian movement would aim not only at taking care of the farmers, but even at drawing some superfluous and unemployed men out of the industrial community and off the consciences of their former employers. Mr. Ford would save the farmers at the expense of his own or somebody else's employees, but an agrarian plan would expect to save the farmers and some of the Ford men too.

———————

I accept in a sense the idea of determinism, and even the Marxian concept of the economic determination of history—except that in naming the precise direction in which society is determined I observe that we are wise chiefly after the event. Historians do better than prophets in telling how the determination works.

This is preliminary to saying that it seems to me arbitrary to assume, as Spengler and many determinists assume, that the whole Western world, but most of all America, is committed to a machine civilization involving factories and mass-production, owners and wage-earners, specialized functions and money as their common denominator, and can now never escape from the consequences. Optimists, of course, do not want to escape from them, thinking the consequences sure to be lovely; others, whose tribe increases, are apprehensive about these consequences. Spengler considers that Western man has built machines stronger than he is and can never master them; whereas Eastern man, symbolized in Gandhi, has refused to have dealings with any machine that the individual cannot control, and will retain his mastery and perhaps ultimately possess the earth. Stuart Chase is alarmed and, I should say, fatalistic about the billion wild horses (they stand for the billion of horsepower) which are running loose in America; who will be able to tame them? The same author visits primitive agrarian Mexico, lovingly observes the self-sufficiency of their simple household and community organization, compares it with our own betrayal of household and community in favor of an economic order bigger than we can understand or control, and declares that the man who would bring the capitalistic economy to Mexico deserves the hottest corner of hell; but remarks as a matter of course that we in the United States have started on our course and can never go back. This last position is a commonplace in our public discussion of economic policy. We are assured that we have picked up the machine and cannot turn it loose; as if an electric current bound our hands to it. But the figure is not apt in describing machinery that now, and periodically, goes dead in our hands.

I do not mean that it is easy for a society as a unit, especially as a democracy, to take effective action in a complicated situation. But I bank on the individual. I think I know his ordinary motives, and his habits of judgment. The individual will drop the machine or get out of it if he finds that he can do it to advantage.

The American farmers ought not to need excessive persuasion to get them out of the capitalistic economy; they need only to believe on historical and economic evidence that another economy will give them security and welfare, and to observe that their present economy after a fair trial has given them only insecurity and the seductive promise of wealth. And if this conversion does not look difficult for farmers, it is certainly not impossible for the unhappy people who have lost contact with the land but who might by an effort recover it. Under these circumstances an agrarian revival seems so much in accord with the logic of events, that I attach little weight to the mysterious predetermination commonly supposed to have seized already upon us all and bound us to the wheel.

I make no prophesies about the future of capitalism in America. The accumulated investment is huge and the habit is strong. It has weathered both stormy seas and mutiny in the ship before now.

The agrarian revival which I covet and the capitalistic system which will keep going are fairly, though not entirely, independent of each other. Questions arise, extremely speculative and of no practical import, like this one: What should be, and will be, the relative proportions of the farm population and the town or industrial population? In a debate at Atlanta against an industrialist I contended that too many farmers had gone off to town, but he rebutted to the effect that not enough of them had done so, and that the farmers would never dispose of their produce until each farmer had three customers in town, or until the ratio of the two populations was 1 to 3. That is as good a guess as another if the farmer, like the townsman, is to operate entirely under the money economy. But in America, where there is land for practically everybody, and will be even when our population becomes stationary at something a little over 150,000,000, as many as like may lead agrarian lives without economic distress, and the ratio might be conceivably very high; it might be 9 to 1. The limit would be the figure beyond which the agrarians would not have left enough people in the cities to supply them with services they needed to supplement their home-made living. A hundred years ago it was something like 3 to 1. A 50-50 division might do very well; but our wishes do not particularly matter. There might conceivably be for some years an exodus from the cities because of their lack of economic opportunity as compared with the land. Then, if the capitalistic economy meanwhile had grown reliable, and tremendously productive, and if perhaps new forms of production demanded additional personnel, the migration citywards might be resumed.

Whatever the distribution of population between the two economies, there would at any rate be an economic dualism in this country; two economies existing side by side. I see nothing startling nor unusual in that; their relations would be perfectly innocent. I can find nothing convincing in the idea that an economic monism is necessarily the destiny ahead of us. That sort of idea is not advanced by realists, but by economists committed to a favorite determinism of their own.

There might even be regionalism in the sense that some regions had gone capitalistic and some had gone agrarian. That possibility likewise does not seem oppressive. There would be a constant to-do in the United States Senate between the champions of the regions, but there is one there usually anyhow. An agrarian South would be scarcely more solid than a Democratic South, and agrarian West scarcely more solid than a Republican West. The principal difference would be that their new names would mean something real.

––––––––––

It should not matter much to the farmers whether the capitalists might or might not approve of their agrarianism, which means virtually their withdrawal from the capitalistic community. But it would be altogether to be expected that the capitalists, when they had thought it over, would approve of some agrarianism in the emergency. There might be a little shame in admitting that capitalism had broken down and could not take care of all its population nor of all its capital, and that America must return in part to a more primitive economy, as if from an experiment that had failed. But the advantages would be too positive for realists to overlook.

For the capitalists are probably both wearied and frightened by the ex-farmers that crowd the doors of the mills and walk the streets of the city looking for employment, and even by the little capitals that come in from the liquidated farm lands looking for safety. The industries are not seeking investors now, nor laborers; both are in horrible excess. The successful capitalists know that hard times will eat up their capital; on them will ultimately be imposed the burden of maintaining the losers, and already they hear ominous rumors about greatly increased taxation or even confiscation at their expense. So far as the farmers can be satisfied with an agrarianism all their own, it means that the responsibility of the capitalists for that much at least of the population is ended.

But it will be better even than that for the harried capitalists. If the present farm population can recover a decent welfare under agrarianism, the exhibit will attract to the farm some of the superfluous men and some of the superfluous capital that now weigh down the industries. Some excess capital will go and bury itself in the land, where it will almost cease to be capital and become the non-competitive and harmless means of subsistence for its owners. And some unwanted men will be removing themselves from the waiting line at the industrial employment offices; and these, in finding their way back to the land, will be as much as signing and delivering to the capitalists a discharge in full from all existing obligations, whether actual or alleged.

———————

Without any particular effort by the state, but wholly through the economic initiative of the individuals concerned, I suggest that an agrarian movement might become massive enough to relieve our staggering capitalistic institutions. Indeed, they might be saved in this way from overwhelming collapse; or they might be saved from the shame and the peril of public appropriation, which is socialism. Let us see finally in just what sense agrarianism is an alternative to socialism.

The true opposite to socialism is individualism. Socialism means public ownership, individualism means private ownership. On the one hand you may leave men alone to their own private devices and let them run their own business as they please; that is individualism. It is the basis on which we in this country have been going hitherto, and they in Europe have been going during our time. On the other hand you may refuse to let the individuals run their business, and have the state take it out of their hands and run it for them. That is the plan the Russians have now undertaken, the first of modern societies to try anything of the kind, though primitive societies may have done it as a matter of course.

But just what kind of economic enterprises have our individuals been trying to carry on for themselves? Latterly they have been remarkably close to unanimous in embarking upon a capitalistic economy; and here we must take note of another pair of opposites, which are simply two varieties of economic technique. *The true opposite of capitalism is agrarianism.* To contrast them once more, agrarianism is the economy of self-sufficient men living on the land and taking subsistence directly from it; old-fashioned and slow, but safe; and quite possible for everybody in the economic society if there is land enough. Capitalism is the economy of men who make not subsistence but money; brilliant when they make much money, as often; immensely more productive than agrarianism because of the principle of specialization, and creative of ingenious goods that are impossible to the other; but risky, because men live only by trade, and are at the mercy of a trading society over which individuals have no control. But both are simply techniques, and if the economic man is a free individual he may elect the one or the other.

And now suppose an economic society of very fixed individualistic principles—individualism is nearly as native to us as breathing—whose members have gone in overwhelmingly for the one or the other technique but are making something less than a success of it, and talk of a change. To be more explicit, suppose that individuals have gone capitalistic, and come to grief, and discuss a change: in what direction will they move? One might expect them to feel that, whatever they did, they would stick to their individualism; and that, if the technique of capitalism had failed them, they had better turn to the techniques of agrarianism. But that is unaccountably not quite the case. So far as their professional economists speak for them, they seem to be saying to themselves, "We will not sacrifice our capitalism to keep our individualism, we will sacrifice our individualism to keep our capitalism." They do not turn to agrarianism, which is the other species of their individualism, but to socialism, under which they would maintain the existing capitalistic system though they ceased to be free individuals.

For, when we say socialism, we have in mind not simply any kind of economy run from start to finish by the state, but a capitalistic economy run that way; a grand layout of mines, factories, railroads, shops, ships, with the state as sole owner, employer, fixer of prices and wages, and general executive. We think of the whole present apparatus of capitalism working on as now but under a different kind of administration. We take socialism to mean state capitalism, and we are being induced little by little to believe that to reach it there is an easy transition from private capitalism.

The rise of modern socialism is a consequence of private capitalism. Karl Marx was evidently a man sensitive to the iniquities of the industrial-capitalistic revolution; but at the same time sensitive to the technical superiority of its processes and its products, else he would not have tried to conserve them. We are beginning generally to consider, under the persuasions of the reformers, that there is no great surface difference between what we call our capitalism and what they call their socialism. They do not propose sabotage and destruction, they want to preserve the whole magnificent productive plant that constitutes our national wealth, modifying only the distribution of its ownership, responsibility, and income. The difference will be an internal one, a moral or psychic one. The same technique, a new private motivation. We shall not be exchanging capitalism for socialism, but individualism for socialism. Private agrarianism to private capitalism to public capitalism—that will have been the order of our progression.

But the attitude of farmers to socialism is very well known: they despise it, they can hardly conceive of it. Between farmers and active socialists is such antipathy that the latter do not even preach to the former, nor look for any converts from that source. This is only in part because socialism comes out of the cities and has on it the odor of soot and of petrol, but no smell of the soil; though that fact does bring it under suspicion. The communistic fury now expressing itself in Russia first captured the poor in the cities, by a natural persuasion, and then had to use stronger methods to capture the kulaks upon the land. The kulaks would have nothing to do with the movement till the movement came to them clothed with authority and penal powers.

The antipathy goes deeper than that. Farmers are fond of money just as city people are, and of the things that money will buy in our present order. They have for that reason gone into the money economy which originated, as well as socialism, in the cities. Why should they not declare for a socialistic state as the way to realize their reasonable desires? It would certainly deal with them as kindly as with any other group, try to furnish them with moderate tasks for their labor and plenty of pretty commodities for their leisure. It may be that the Soviet Republic does not yet shower blessings upon the laborers whom it has ordered to its collectivist farms, but eventually it hopes to do better by them. Why are not farmers, like others who have been unsuccessful in the scramble, anxious to see the highly productive machinery set to working in their real interests? I should like to think they are not deeply infatuated with the products of this machinery, but prepared to believe that these have been somewhat overestimated, and willing to take something much simpler and homelier as nearly as good. But I do not risk that assumption; the farmers too have tasted of the fruit of the tree. Again, it would be pleasant to assume that farmers are too shrewd to be taken in quickly by its economic prospects of success; but I do not suppose they have such a vastly superior economic intuition for detecting the weaknesses in the system. Farmers like the products of capitalism, and farmers hardly know any special reason why they could not enjoy them under socialism.

The difference between farmers and others is that they know better what individualism means. It is their great luxury, and tastes sweeter than most material commodities. The present money farmer is hardly the same individualist that the old agrarian farmer was, but he is a better one than most of the cogs in the capitalistic machine. Though he works for money, he works in his own way and at his own discretion. He is not a controlled and directed man, not responsible to his stockholders, running his modest business very much by himself, and intending to keep on running it that way. The Russian kulaks ran little businesses which were fairly wretched, but over the orders of their new masters they have been so stubbornly insistent on continuing to run them that terms simply could not be made with them, and they have had to be impressed into virtual slavery by multitudes. They lacked the gift for collectivism. Our own farmers, and I for one say it to their credit, have in their constitution a good deal of the kulak prejudice. They never manage to organize for collective effort even when they want to, and are quite behind other groups in this respect. They relish the idea of deciding in the morning what they will do during the day; an unusual occupation privilege. If they choose, they may even spend the day doing nothing at all, which is the prerogative of few men in the civilized world, and much too fine to be generally recommended. Nobody else who is seriously engaged in business has anything like so much freedom. They are the most incorrigible individualists in our society, and this is reinforced if it is not caused by the nature of their occupation.

Therefore agrarianism will appeal to farmers as socialism will not. And therefore, if ever the socialist state hangs even in the balance not knowing whether to be or not to be, the antagonism of the country population will be the decisive factor in its rejection. And if there were no other fault to be found in this country to the Five Year Plan, we would hate it and scorn to emulate it because of the treatment it has had to mete out the kulaks.[10]

10. Economic plan implemented by Joseph Stalin in 1928.

THE STATE AND THE LAND

Countries like Germany and England are hit hard at a time of fierce international competition for markets; they have learned to rely for life on those markets. Each has a producing plant, with its population nicely allocated to the plant, which cannot run without heavy foreign trade; when the trade breaks down, the country suffers. But it is strange if our economists would still have us dreaming and working for a great development of our own foreign trade—emulating the England of a century ago, the Germany of half a century ago. Do they not see where that policy has brought England and Germany, now that overproduction is worldwide and here to stay? And do they think that there is no other economy open to us?

So fixed is our idea that we have a future in international trade that we have embarked on the program of extending credits to embarrassed nations, in order to smooth the waters and restore trade quickly. We keep them productive at a time of general overproduction. Our economists latterly are pretty well agreed that this is an impossible program to undertake for the benefit of individuals. Nevertheless, the leading idea of our foreign policy just now is to save Europe without the liquidation of a single nation.

Originally published in *The New Republic*, February 17, 1932.

We would never have thought of saving Europe if we had been right and sound at home. The foreign markets offered by a saved Europe are expected to save our hugely overproductive society from itself. Our domestic economy is out of balance: the production side being consistently far ahead of the consumption side. So we are desperate, we will try anything, even to the saving of Europe, if it promises to find us new purchasers and right the balance. But our producing plant is 30 to 50 percent idle; and all the foreign markets in the world, the European included, have at best taken but a tenth of our production. What incredible piece of luck do we expect from trading with a saved Europe? If we go at the foreign trade ruthlessly and expertly enough and really succeed in so underselling our competitors as to get back to producing at full capacity—to say nothing of expanding this capacity— we will ruin Europe faster than we can save it, and having ruined Europe we will have cooked our goose. The name of that policy is economic imperialism, and no policy could look much vainer or more dangerous. If on the other hand we should join, as is barely conceivable, in some international program of rationalization, we shall have to see the world markets allocated among the nations on the basis of their actual equipment for production and our own quota will offer an insignificant degree of salvation to our producers.

Let those nations whose populations must live by a foreign trade fight to the death to get it and hold it, as indeed they will and must. But we are not in that position; we are incomparably stronger. We are not as Britain, nor Germany, nor Italy, nor even France. Our economic distinction is a great one and a simple one; it consists in the fact that we have plenty of land. Does that mean nothing to the political economist? It ought to mean an important instrument of national policy. Through the land we may save our population at home, we may stabilize our economy, we may remain quite independent of an international competition which is bound to break more nations than it can possibly make.

There are 200,000 miners in Britain who have not entered a mine since the War, and are reasonably certain never to enter a mine again. But suppose there were an abundance of cheap land available in in Britain. Would any intelligent ministry, harassed with the task of keeping them and their families alive, spend half an hour in deciding to colonize them and thus to take them off the public treasury?

We have no group of unemployed in this country perhaps quite so miserable as the British miners. But we do have problems of the identical sort. We can see clearly now what a capitalistic economy has done for us. It has bestowed upon us a great aggregate wealth, but with this good, or following this good, comes increasingly an evil that it does not seem possible to eradicate. In capitalism there is an inherent tendency to excessive investment out of income, causing overcapitalization and overproduction. This means, on the part of the capitalists, the waste of their capitals, and sometimes the total extinction of them. But for the workers who were attached to these capitals it means something rather worse—unemployment and plain destitution. And these evils do not wait for a great business collapse to reveal themselves, either; they attend constantly upon capitalism, even in its very impulse toward greater efficiency. For its new machines are continually evicting men from its factories; and its improvements in organization, both vertical and horizontal, are continually evicting middlemen and small owners and personnel. Altogether, capitalism is causing the producing society to grow more and more exclusive, which means, incidentally, that the purchasing society must grow more exclusive too. Both capitalists and wage earners are in excess, and the surplus constitutes a body of reputed citizens whom our economic society cannot assimilate. They are on the consciences of our statesmen; and no wonder these latter look yearningly at Europe, to see if there is no way to put them to work producing for a foreign trade. But they are looking in the wrong direction.

———————

How then is the land to save us? In this simple sense: those who have lost their places in our ordinary capitalistic society may begin all over upon the land, rather in the manner of their pioneer forbears if necessary, and take their living not from a capitalistic community but directly from the bounty of nature. In that position they are free, independent, economically immortal.

We must make a clear-cut distinction between two land economies: a modern *capitalistic* or money economy, and a much older *agrarian* economy. It is not by applying capitalism to the land that we can help ourselves; we have lately been trying that with all our might and know it to be a mistake. The capitalistic landowner conceives his land as a factory, producing goods exclusively for sale, and himself as the sort of consumer who must buy with money all that he consumes. The trouble with farming on that basis is that the industry is even more overcapitalized than others. The owners get a smaller return (if they do not get a negative one) and the wage earners get a smaller wage. All the farm land in this country is a capital ready if we please to produce for a market; always enough of it is actually producing to glut the market and ruin the business. Nothing will save the farmers in the sense of enabling them to sell all the produce they can raise. Our experiment with a Federal Farm Board, which tried on a modest scale to do something of the sort, would have written into our economic history quite its most ridiculous chapter, except that it has at least offered a demonstration which was really required by many people of the hopelessness of saving the farms as a pure industry or as a form of capitalism.

An agrarian economy does not conceive of the land as a capital to earn with, not primarily at least; but as a direct source of subsistence for its population. This is the most ancient of economies, which many times has proved its validity. It persisted very largely in this country until about two generations ago, and in some places, as in the South, it still occasionally persists. Pioneers and frontiersmen practiced it almost exclusively. Colonies of German or Swiss or other immigrants are capable to this day of taking mediocre American land and erecting on it a sound economic community with hardly the use of a dollar.

But generally, in complex societies, the farmers have mixed their primary agrarian economy with some capitalistic economy too; they have made a living with their own hands first, and then they have made their money crops on the side. After all the industrial, professional and urban populations have to be fed; and after all, their services, while not quite indispensable, are desirable for people generally, including farmers; and nothing is more natural than exchange. But half the total effort of the farmers is more than plenty to furnish this market, and the rest of it must go to furnishing themselves. It will be hard to dispute the following as a proposition in economics: the farmers, if they will put their agrarian economy above their money economy, may have about all the money they are now making and most of their own living besides.

Farming today ought to be easier than it used to be, because the technique has improved. Economists of the most realistic sort are needed to give new body and practical detail to an agrarian recovery. But spiritual leaders are needed too, to emphasize the value of full-blooded agrarian living as compared with the technical and rather routine lives that most of us are obliged to lead under the capitalistic dispensation. Our old agrarian practice created a manner of life which was individualistic, dignified and full of esthetic satisfactions. There is no danger for the present in overdoing this side of the appeal. Capitalism has always hurt some of us spiritually, and now pinches many of us physically, and for both reasons it is time for a considerable defection from an economy to which we subscribed too unanimously and too earnestly.

It is easy to prophesy that those who are already on the land are going to stay there; there is no place for them to go. And they are being forced by economic pressure, for the most part without indulging in any theory about it whatever, to fall into agrarian ways once more; into providing gardens, orchards, chicken-yards, smokehouses, dairy cows; even into repairing their tumble-down habitations, seeing they are going to be there a long time. It is not very daring to predict also that more and more of the ex-farmers, having met with a chilly welcome from the capitalistic world, will find their way back to the land. That movement too has begun. Let us remark that if this movement means only another money-making venture, with land as the capital, it is a movement from the frying-pan into the fire.

But there are many whom economic logic would send back to the land that cannot get back on logic alone; they cannot un-aided even find today's bread, much less transportation and tools and land. Should they be aided by the state, acting advisedly to formulate and finance a general agrarian program?

I shall not venture to claim that the state should immediately act toward this end. Our economists and statesmen are evidently not convinced that the state needs to do anything yet for the relief of its surplus of citizens. But we shall soon know better whether there is actually with us a considerable body of the "permanently unemployed"—melancholy phrase, officially sanctioned for the first time recently by the President of the United States, who is reported to have used it in considering the general problem of unemployment relief.[1] But when and if the state does undertake to use the public moneys for such relief, the most rational dis-position of them will be in settling upon the land those who are to be relieved. Relief through charitable doles may be humanitar-ian but it is not economic, it does not cure; this month's dole is of no effect in preventing next month's. Nor is relief through public-construction projects any better; if the projects were sound, they ought to be constructed anyway; if they are not, they may become as extensive as the Pyramids, and still fresh projects will be neces-sary to take care of the unemployed next season. There is but one way to make the beneficiaries, these derelicts of a capitalistic so-ciety, into self-sustaining and self-supporting citizens: by inducting them into an agrarian economy.

How would the state proceed? In Denmark the method which was successfully employed for half a century, and abandoned only when all the land was filled up with small owners, was for the state to finance the purchase of land for the indigent purchasers. That is the easiest way. Another way would be for the state to buy up and keep on hand a great deal of land, which is plentiful and cheap, for homesteading. This way might involve machinery, red tape and bureaucracy. But it would have the great advantage that the state could satisfy itself better that the land was being occupied for

1. Herbert Hoover.

genuine agrarian purposes, not for money-cropping. The state could assist in the development of real agrarian communities, and lend the instruction of its expert economists. We have had in this country a great deal of experience with homesteading; and though this would be a very elaborate kind of homesteading, there are probably no appalling difficulties.

But without an agrarian movement, whether private or official, we in our capitalistic economy are drifting into an impossible situation, like that of Europe, and the only way we shall get out of it is by abandoning our individualistic code of ethics, which is bred in the bone, and substituting socialistic devices. I imagine that Americans would prefer some agrarianism. The moralists ought to be pleased with it, and the capitalists themselves, now bearing the brunt of taxation and threatened with annihilation, ought to be delighted. The objections will come from professional economists, insulated in their capitalistic communities and having never heard of agrarianism; and from professional publicists who have conceived such a grudge against capitalism that nothing will stop them from killing it, even if in doing so they must kill the Western conscience too.

JOHN CROWE RANSOM

JOHN CROWE RANSOM (1888–1974) was an American poet and critic whose book *The New Criticism* (1941) provided the name of the influential mid-twentieth-century school of criticism. He taught English at Vanderbilt University and at Kenyon College, where he founded and edited the literary magazine *The Kenyon Review*. He published numerous volumes of poetry, including *Selected Poems* (1945, 1969), which won a National Book Award.

JASON PETERS is professor of English and the Dorothy J. Parkander Chair in Literature at Augustana College.

Lightning Source UK Ltd.
Milton Keynes UK
UKHW010856230622
404821UK00002B/134